GOD'S POWER IS FOR YOU

Other Books by Wesley L. Duewel:

Touch the World Through Prayer (A challenging manual
on prayer that has become a bestseller)

Let God Guide You Daily (A manual that helps you
enter into the joy of God's guidance as the daily
experience of life)

Ablaze for God (A book to challenge Christian workers
and lay leaders to Spirit-empowered life and service)

Mighty Prevailing Prayer (A guide to intensified
intercession and prayer warfare)

Measure Your Life (Seventeen ways God is measuring
your life as He prepares your eternal reward)

Revival Fire (The thrilling story of God's mighty
working in revivals, especially since the time
of Wesley and Whitefield)

GOD'S POWER IS FOR YOU

Reflections on the Deeper Life

Wesley L. Duewel

ZondervanPublishingHouse
Grand Rapids, Michigan

A Division of HarperCollins*Publishers*

God's Power Is for You
Copyright © 1997 by Wesley L. Duewel

Requests for information should be addressed to:

ZondervanPublishingHouse
Grand Rapids, Michigan 49530

Library of Congress Cataloging-in-Publication Data

Duewel, Wesley L.
   God's power is for you / Wesley L. Duewel.
      p. cm.
   ISBN 0-310-21144-1 (pbk.)
    1. Christian life. 2. Power (Christian theology). 3. Meditations. I. Title.
BV4501.2.D7366 1997
242—dc21   96-46345
                                                CIP

Interior design by Sue Vandenberg Koppenol

Printed in the United States of America

97 98 99 00 01 02 03 04 /❖ DH/ 10 9 8 7 6 5 4 3 2 1

Contents

To My Readers

Do you hunger—

To be more Spirit-filled?
To be more used of God?
To see a heaven-sent revival?
To have the Holy Spirit search your heart in order to bless you more?
To have a prayer life used by God?
To bring joy to God and blessing to others?

If so, this book is for you.

These meditations and reflections were written over a twelve-year period, conceived and born out of much prayer. May God make them a blessing to you.

Open Your Life to God

Open your heart and let God flood your whole being with His life, His love, and His power. Open your heart and let God make you a greater example of His grace, a more effective instrument in His service, and a greater channel of blessing than ever before. There is no limit to what God can do in you and through you if your whole being is absolutely open to possession by God, to the will of God, and to work for God.

God is waiting for the open door, the open heart, and the open life. There is no hesitation on God's part. God has no better time than today. In this regard it is not proper to say to God, "If it be Your will." We know it is His will to possess us completely, to fill us with His very self, and to glorify Himself through us. This is the goal of the Incarnation. This is the whole purpose of redemption. This is God's will, this is God's time. He is just waiting for us to open the door.

Each human being needs to open his heart to Christ the Savior and let Him come into his life. Each child of God needs to make a total, once-for-all surrender of his whole life, his innermost self; yes, all that he is, for time and eternity. He must thus let God the Holy Spirit cleanse him, fill him, and empower him.

Only an absolute surrender, an uttermost consecration will bring you the fullness of God's Spirit in all His lordship and power. But no crisis experience, however indispensable and however complete, can provide such a once-for-all opening of your being to God that no further opening of yourself and giving of yourself to God is ever necessary.

You can make such an absolute surrender of your will to God that henceforth it will not be you but Christ living in you. You can live with daring abandon as one who has been crucified with Christ. One can become so dead to self and the world that, cost what it may, no situation is ever again faced with anything less than a willingness and joyful eagerness to obey. But is that true of you? If so, that is a great beginning.

Your whole life must be one of utter dedication to God, of personal sanctification through the indwelling and enabling of the Holy Spirit. Such a life opens the door to the holy romance and adventure of a life ever more and more open to God. Nothing less than this can fully and truly satisfy God or you.

The life transfigured and empowered by the indwelling Spirit in His fullness must be daily presented to God ever more intelligently and eagerly. The first thing to do on awakening in the morning is to open your whole being anew to God. Thank God for the glorious yesterday of His indwelling and open your being unreservedly to God for His indwelling throughout your new day.

You have not sinned against Him during your sleep; of course not. If you were victorious when you went to sleep, then you are victorious now whether you feel like it or not. But welcome God anew each new day. Tell Him again how fully you belong to Him, how ready and eager you are to obey Him, and how you long and yearn for Him. Tell Him how much you love Him. Tell Him over and over again.

As you go about your work or when you have leisure moments during your day, open your whole being to God. Look up into His face, even if it be only for a moment. Smile in His face with a loving smile. Rejoice in His love. Thank Him for His love. Ask Him to keep filling you more and more. Ask Him what you can do to give Him more joy. Praise Him. Love Him. Adore Him. Sing to Him. Bless Him. Thank Him.

Live in unbroken communion. Live in constant eager obedience. And all the while just keep rejoicing in His love, opening your whole being to all of His Being. Without your realizing it, you will be deepening your walk with God and enlarging your capacity for fellowship with God. You will be making more sweet, more natural, and more wonderful your moment-by-moment communion with the Lord.

God is waiting for your spiritual capacity to increase so He can flood your innermost being with more and more of Himself. He is longing for your spiritual sight to grasp more and more of the beauty, the glory, and the wonder of His Being. He is eagerly waiting for the opportunity to reveal Himself within you and through you.

The plan of redemption has been completed; the price has been paid once and for all. But oh, how the Lord longs and waits to work it out more and more in your life and through your life. Perhaps you have not yet caught the vision of the person of God that He plans and waits for you to become. Perhaps you have not yet glimpsed His incomparably great power for you as you believe (Eph. 1:19). If not, just open yourself to Him more and more.

Seize with joyful eagerness and loving expectation every opportunity you get for private prayer, for waiting before the Lord, and for rejoicing in His love. Who knows what God is just about to reveal to you? Who knows what blessed communion is waiting for you? Every time you enter into the house of God or into some Christian meeting or service, yearn and hunger, rejoice and expect to meet God. Welcome His presence again; open yourself to Him anew.

Every time you see an opportunity to serve Him, to bless others, to suffer for Him, or share His cross—run to obey. Thank Him and ask Him to use you. Open your heart, open your life, open your time, open your prejudices, open your fearful nature, and open yourself wider and wider to all that God can be to you.

Forget about yourself. Forget about your personal interests. Forget about what others think and say and how they act. A few

moments worrying about others will rob you of hours of blessedness. You can't afford to stoop to such things. Just keep opening
yourself to God. Live for God and rejoice in the Lord. Miracle life,
miracle love, and miracle power are waiting to flood every aspect of
your life and every avenue of your being. God is coming in all His
fullness and power. Just open yourself more and more and praise
Him, love Him, and rejoice.

Lord, I open my whole life to You today.

Incomparably Great Power

2

The Holy Spirit is the author of your hunger for more of God's power in your life. The prayer He inspired Paul to pray is the echo of the heart-cry of God—that you may know "his incomparably great power for us who believe" (Eph. 1:19). More than half of Paul's prayer is given to describing this power. It is an incomparably great power, a mighty power, a resurrection power, a power by which Christ reigns over all—and all this power is for you. Weymouth translates this as "the transcendent greatness of His power in us." Williams translates it "power for us." Power for us, power in us—this is God's will for you and me.

You will never be constantly victorious until this power indwells you. Till then you will never be able to say with Paul, "Thanks be to God, who always leads us in triumphal procession in Christ" (2 Cor. 2:14). The purpose of God's power is always to lead us triumphantly. The tragedy of our lives is our spiritual weakness; the tragedy of our ministry is its spiritual ineffectiveness. Is it power or the lack of power that is most characteristic of your spiritual life?

The average Christian makes one primary mistake. Thousands pray for power to come upon them; God's plan is for power to indwell you. It is not an external, added power for you to use; it is an internal, transforming power by which God can use you. The Holy Spirit does not merely come upon you; He comes within you. His baptism is not an external baptism upon you; it is a burning baptism of fire within you. The fullness of His presence is not proved by a transient gift, but by His abiding, transforming, empowering, indwelling. Gifts are additional; His purifying, anointing, empowering presence within you is essential. "The anointing you received from him remains in you" (1 John 2:27). In God's order, abiding purity must precede abiding power. God's priority is first the power to be, then the power to do. The reason God can entrust us with so little of His power is that we are too full of self.

Are you hungry for the power of the Holy Spirit? This hunger is God-given. It shows you the need in your Christian life. God has promised this power to you (Acts 2:39). It will be proved by His power within your daily life. This means power to love, power to be Christlike and holy. Hungry heart, God gave you that hunger because He wants to satisfy you. The power that raised Christ from the dead is the power of the Holy Spirit. The Holy Spirit wants to work in you as surely as He worked in raising Christ. When the Holy Spirit crucifies self in your life, you too will be able to testify with Paul that it is no longer you, but Christ living in you (Gal. 2:20). Thank God for your hunger, and trust Him to fulfill His promise to do the incomparably great within your life.

Lord, deepen my hunger for Your holy power.

By This All Will Know 3

Love must show in your words, in your face, in the very way you meet with and serve all those around you. Love must be proved in your attitudes and actions. We need a revival of love to sweep through all our churches till every misunderstanding, every quarrel, and every hard feeling against a fellow Christian is forgiven and forgotten. This is the revival we need—a revival of forgiving, healing, all-conquering love in every home, every Christian institution, every local church.

The greatest testimony we will ever give is the Christlike love we show among ourselves and to others. Of course, we must love the unsaved and prove our love to them; we must serve them with love. But Christ emphasized the powerful witness of mutual love among believers: "By this all men will know that you are my disciples, if you love one another" (John 13:35).

Love must not quarrel, love must not hold resentment, love must not answer evil with evil. Love must not fight, bite, and devour. Love must not react unkindly, impatiently, or ungraciously to any deed of injustice or any hard word of others. These are all negative attitudes and actions. Love must not do any of these things, but love is far more than abstaining and not doing. Love is positive. Love is active.

Christlike love is a love that longs to express itself. It longs to bless in every possible way. It longs for the good of others. It longs to comfort and help others and to reach out in every way it can to make itself known. Christlike love seeks opportunities to speak, to smile, to love.

When Christians meet together, they should so rejoice to see each other that anyone watching them will be able to see their joy in their faces. There should be smiles and cheerful words for the children. There should be looks of recognition and words of appreciation and encouragement for the youth. There should be looks of loving and sincere fellowship, words of loving interest, and genuine goodwill for all.

Whenever Christians meet together Christian love should cause everyone to feel encouraged, strengthened, and reassured of sympathy, prayer, and cooperation. Every gathering should be marked by every Christian's alertness for any opportunity to express his Christian love and to help and encourage others. No one should be overlooked; no one should be ignored. No one should be able to enter a Christian service and leave as a stranger.

The whole gathering should be marked by rejoicing in one another, thanking God for one another, and expressing positive love to one another. There should be an intimate, mutual concern so that anyone's burdens will become the burdens of all, anyone's sorrows will become the sorrows of all, and anyone's joys will become the joys of all. Every church gathering should be a communion of the saints. Coldness on the part of anyone should be so noticeable that everyone will begin to pray for that person so that full fellowship will be quickly restored.

Christian love should be evident by the daily prayers of each Christian for the other Christians of the group and by daily prayers for those who are ill, tempted, or in need. The conversation at mealtime should be one of such genuine appreciation and love for other Christians that the children of the family will be eager to meet the people their parents have spoken of. Not one word of criticism or unkindness should ever be breathed within the family group.

A Christian family should be so characterized by love that it stands out as a different kind of family. The Christian home should be so filled with love that for the whole community it is a light that cannot be hidden. It should reach out in fellowship to all the other Christian homes; it should reach out in service to any home, Christian or non-Christian, where there is sickness or need.

This was the love that bound the early church together. This was the love that caused the pagans to say of the church of the first three centuries, "Behold, how they love one another!" This was the kind of love that Christ knew would be the most powerful testimony to the reality of His grace and salvation.

Such love makes others hungry to know the secret of the joy and fellowship in our lives. Such love impresses others until they have no evil they can truthfully say about us. Such love makes itself felt so strongly that even when we are falsely accused, the people around us will know that the accusations against us cannot be true.

The early church grew and spread by its witness and by its love. Its love for Christ was a joyous reality. Its love for Christ was proved in the members' overflowing love for one another. No one could see it and fail to be impressed by it. The Christians loved each other so much that they shared their money and goods with each other. They went from house to house fellowshiping, eating, praying, and rejoicing together.

And they won others by their love. The hardest thing to fight is love. It is not merely a way of tolerance. Love suffers and still loves and serves. Love not only endures silently but blesses the hand that strikes it; it yearns for and blesses the one who persecutes. This is a love that can come only from Christ.

Such love cannot be hidden. It cannot be forgotten. It cannot be avoided. This love will not let go until it wins; it will not give up even to the point of death. It is the most effective witness that God can give to man. Lord, give us a revival of this love. Lord, flood our churches and institutions with this love. Lord, pour this love into our hearts by the Holy Spirit (Rom. 5:5).

To be filled with the Spirit means to be filled with this love. To possess the fruit of the Spirit means to possess this love. This is the love that triumphs in spite of Satan's strategies. By this all people will know—when we love as Christ loves.

Lord, make my love visible and Christlike.

First Things First

It is so easy for us to shift the things of first importance in our lives to second or third place. Each birthday challenges us to evaluate our life's stewardship and relationships. The arrival of each anniversary calls to immediate attention the fact that our responsibilities have increased and the time remaining for us to fulfill these obligations has decreased.

If we are ever to make an impact on others for God, we have no time to lose. God has invested mercy, grace, and repeated blessings in our lives. You and I have been blessed beyond our deserving. God is expecting us to be faithful stewards of all He has given us. The time is coming when He will say to you and me, "Give an account of your management" (Luke 16:2).

Life is not measured by the number of years we have lived. Life is not measured by how busy we have been during those years. Our life on earth will be examined in the light of eternity. Everyone's work will have to pass through God's test of fire. That which is of eternal value will abide, and all else will be consumed by the fire (1 Cor. 3:12–15). The question is not how much we do, but how we do what we do. Ten hours of hard labor with a weak prayer foundation will probably not have the eternal value of one hour

of labor on a strong foundation of prayer. Ten sermons that lack
the anointing of God's Holy Spirit will not be equal to one sermon that has His mighty anointing.

> *Little is much, if God is in it.*
> *Man's earthly hour is not worth God's minute.*
> *But much is little everywhere*
> *If God the labor does not share.*
> *So work with God; then nothing's lost;*
> *Who works with Him does best and most.*
>
> Author unknown

There is always a danger of valuing our work for God more
than God Himself. There is danger in treasuring God's gifts more
than God the Giver, in spending much time with God's people but
little time with God, in being busy rather than contemplative. A
birthday is a time to evaluate our lives to see how satisfactorily they
measure up to God's standard.

How many things of secondary value are consuming your
time and energy and robbing you of God's best? How many legit-
imate things are robbing you of God's richest blessings? You are free.
You can choose what fills your life and occupies your time and
thoughts. But if you fail to put first things first in your life, you
will be missing something throughout eternity.

How long will you live? How much of your life's work is
already in the past? May God help you and me to live totally for
God. Our lives will mean more for God when we spend them more
fully with Him. Do we dare to rid our lives of the secondary and
the transient? Pause before you go further and ask God to help
you put Him first in your life from today on.

Father, teach me to always keep You first in my life.

God Loves the World 5

God loves the whole world. He loves because He is love (1 John 4:8). How superficial is our understanding of this tremendous truth! It is His deepest nature to love infinitely, constantly, and personally. And His love is infinite so that He can love every other person just as fully as He loves us.

God loves the world so much that He wants us to share as fully as possible in that same love. The more you love the world, the more intimate His love to you becomes, the more joy you bring to Him, and the greater the reward He plans and prepares for you to experience throughout eternity.

The greatest way you can show your gratitude to God for His saving you is for you to take more and more of the peoples of the world into your heart and into your loving arms of prayer. The more you love Him, the more you will love them. The more you love them, the more you will experience His love for you.

Two great commandments are closely and beautifully interrelated. As you love God with all your heart, soul, mind, and strength (Luke 10:27–28), you will love the people He loves, and you will love your neighbor as yourself. What you do for those He loves, even for the least of them, you really do for Jesus (Matt. 25:34–

45). Everything you do to serve a needy one you do as serving Jesus. Jesus' heart leaps for joy every time you plead and pray for the unsaved. He hungers so infinitely for their salvation that when you also really hunger and thirst for their salvation you become unspeakably precious to Jesus. Nothing makes you more special to Him.

There is a constant, gnawing pain in the heart of God because so many millions of people are still unreached. Why is it that there are still places where thousands of people live but where there has been no regular witnessing to them of Jesus' love and death for them? They have no concept of what it means to be saved from sin.

It is the Holy Spirit who has given us a heart that responds to human need. When we see a lovely child and our heart goes out to her in love, let us think of how much more the heart of Jesus loves her and longs for her to be saved. The Spirit helps us feel a little of this great love in the heart of Jesus. When your heart is pained to see young boys and men with the hardening marks of sin already on their faces, think of how much more the heart of Jesus is pained. The Holy Spirit is helping you feel just a bit of what so intensely pains the heart of Christ.

Then multiply this divine compassion for one unsaved person by the millions and millions of people on earth. Think of the overwhelming sorrow that pains the heart of Christ. If not even a sparrow falls to the ground without God's knowing it (Matt. 10:29), think of all the burdens and pains that sweep over the heart of God every day as He looks down upon our tragic world. God sees all. He knows all. He loves all. He longs to save and help all. God desires that no one miss heaven and be eternally lost.

When you begin to love the world for Christ's sake and when you begin to understand the burden on the heart of God and the pain that pierces His loving heart each day, you will begin to develop a new and more earnest prayer life. You will begin to grieve for the sins that so deeply grieve the heart of God. You will begin to share the heartbeat of Jesus.

God loves the world so much that there is room in His heart for everyone. Let Him reveal this love to you more fully than ever before. Kneel at His feet and let Him show you the need of the world as He sees it and feels it. Ask Him to give you eyes that see as He sees and a heart that hungers as He hungers. Then your out-poured intercession will echo some of the intercession of Jesus and your ever-deepening united intercession (Jesus' and yours) will thrill His heart and yours.

Lord, help me understand and share Your great love, and may it transform my prayer life.

The Overcoming Life

No eye has ever seen, no ear has ever heard, and the heart of man has never fully comprehended the length, the breadth, and the depth of the love of God. Undoubtedly no saint has ever experienced, no tongue has ever fully extolled, and few children of God, if any, have ever fully glimpsed the victory, the radiance, and the glory that God longs to make a part of the common experience of His children.

Every hunger in your heart, every deep prayer too inexpressible in words, every glow of expectancy stirred in your heart by the promises of God are proofs of the reality and greatness of the overcoming life to which God calls you.

Surely the average Christian life is not what God wants the normal Christian life to be. No church or Christian organization can claim that all its members are spiritually pure, victorious, radiant, and mature. However, there are Christians whose lives are so filled with the love of God, so victorious over sin, and so indwelt by the fullness of God's Holy Spirit that their walk with God is as far above the "average" Christian life as the "average" Christian is above the level of the unregenerate but moral sinners.

It is tragic that so much of our Christian living is incongruous with New Testament promises, commands, and examples. It is tragic that the manifestation of "self" in its various carnal forms is marring the witness, the fruitfulness, and the Christlikeness of so many who nevertheless know that they were truly born of God and have experienced His transforming power and forgiveness. It is also tragic that those who are conscious of repeated defeats in their personal lives are too prejudiced to believe in the possibility of an undefeated life or to accept the testimony of some who have experienced a deep and abiding crucifixion of self.

However, there are definite reasons for these prejudices. Many who can testify to victory have suffered numerous defeats. Others have mixed their testimony of victory with an unscriptural emphasis on and association with manifestations of what they claim to be spiritual power and spiritual gifts. Many have testified to a high level of spiritual attainment yet have not demonstrated a life of constant growth, increasing radiance, and spiritual attractiveness. They still lack overflowing love and spiritual glow.

For too many, a life of victory, though it has included victory over many or all outward manifestations of sin, has been comparatively static and surprisingly fruitless. Such people have been gloriously satisfied with personal blessing until this satisfaction has become a snare. It has become their goal rather than a foundation on which to build.

Others have become discouraged or embittered. They have discovered how superficial some of their so-called victories have been. They have mistaken holy emotions for spiritual deliverance. They have become aware that their purity and victory are not as complete as they had supposed, and instead of gaining the courage to press on until they fully experience all that the Bible promises, they presume that they have misunderstood the Bible's promise, and that a defeated life is a normal Christian life.

Satan has tricked them into becoming self-defensive; thus they doubt the testimonies of those who have experienced the glory of a truly Spirit-cleansed, Spirit-filled, and Spirit-led life. Satan has tricked them into believing that God's commands and promises

refer to an unattainable ideal rather than to the life to which He
actually calls them.

Are you a satisfied Christian? Are you an overcoming Christian? Are you really a Spirit-filled Christian? Are you willing to
humble yourself, confess your need, and obey God regardless of
the cost? If you could obtain an all-loving, all-triumphant, overcoming life, a life filled to overflowing with all the fullness of God,
would you be willing to do whatever God requires of you?

Lord, open my eyes to all the spiritual victory and glo-
ries Your death and resurrection have provided for me.

God Works for Those Who Wait 7

Oh, that God would demonstrate His mighty power in your life and in your work! Oh, that a new day may dawn for you! Oh, that the long-delayed prayer-answer that you have longed for from God for years may suddenly be yours! Oh, that God would rend the heavens and come down to work in your behalf! Are those not the longings of your heart? Take courage, Christian, God wants to do these mighty works in your life. He not only wants to do so but He also will do so if you wait.

Isaiah poured out his heart in a passion of prayer: "Oh, that you would rend the heavens and come down" (Isa. 64:1). He had an unutterable longing to see God work. He knew it was time for God to work; he knew that God could demonstrate His miracle-working power. But why was the answer to his prayer so delayed?

Suddenly Isaiah knew the answer to his own question. God, he says, will act for me if I persevere in prayer. "Since ancient times no one has heard, no ear has perceived, no eye has seen any God besides you, who acts on behalf of those who wait for him" (Isa. 64:4).

This was the same answer God had revealed to Isaiah some fourteen years earlier: "He gives strength to the weary and increases the power of the weak. . . . but those who hope in the Lord will renew

27

their strength. They will soar on wings like eagles; they will run and not grow weary, they will walk and not be faint" (Isa. 40:29, 31).

God works for those who wait. God works *in* them, *through* them, and *for* them. God gives them power, and He increases and renews their strength. God works *in* those who wait. He is able to do "immeasurably more than all we ask or imagine, according to his power that is at work within us" (Eph. 3:20). God also causes us to soar on wings like eagles, to run without weariness, and to walk on and on till we reach God's chosen destination (Isa. 40:31). He goes with us and fulfills His holy purposes through us. God works *through* those who wait. Thanks be to His wonderful name, He will also work *for* those who wait. If we put His interests first, He will put our interests on His priority list.

"Delight yourself in the Lord and he will give you the desires of your heart. Commit your way to the Lord; trust in him and he will do this. . . . Be still before the Lord and wait patiently for him" (Ps. 37:4–5, 7). Believe it! Believe it! Don't be discouraged; God will work on your behalf. Just rejoice in Him, stop worrying; and start believing and praising. His words to you are "delight yourself," "commit," "rest," and "wait patiently." You have the privilege and the right to prove His promises true.

This waiting that Isaiah and the psalmist speak of is not the passive, indifferent waiting of one who does not care. It is, rather, the waiting that involves believing, rejoicing, praising worship. It is the waiting of one who expects great things from God and attempts great things for God. You must take time to delight yourself in the Lord. You must take time to worship and praise Him. Your prayer must not be one of despair, but a prayer of happy expectation. God will work if you wait, so be sure to wait.

What would you have God do for you? What do you really long for most deeply? Do you think God wants you to be disappointed? Do you fear He has forgotten to be gracious? Never! Be bold enough to ask God for all that you need and desire. Then expect Him to work; keep believing, praising, and prevailing in prayer. God will work in you, through you, and for you as you wait.

Do you remember the following hymn?

Unanswered yet, the prayer your lips have pleaded
In agony of heart these many years.
Does faith begin to fail? Is hope departed
And think you all in vain those falling tears?
Say not the Father has not heard your prayer;
You shall have your desire, sometime, somewhere.

Unanswered yet, but do not say ungranted;
Perhaps your part is not yet wholly done.
The work began when first your prayer was uttered
And God will finish what He hath begun.
If you will keep the incense burning there
You shall have your desire, sometime, somewhere.

Unanswered yet? Faith cannot be unanswered;
Her feet are firmly planted on the rock.
Amid the wildest storms, she stands undaunted,
Nor quails beneath the wildest thunder shock.
She knows Omnipotence has heard her prayer
And cries, "It shall be done, sometime, somewhere."

Ophelia G. Adams

∞

Teach me, Lord, to wait.

It Is No Secret
What God Can Do

For many years a godly father and mother prayed for their wayward son to be saved. The father was widely known as a strong evangelical leader and was elected bishop by his denomination. He was a member of the Home Board of OMS International (a missionary society to which I have already given fifty-six years of my life). But in spite of the exemplary lives and the prayers of his parents, Stuart seemed to go farther and farther away from God. He became a well-known Hollywood figure, having had a radio program for twenty-one years, and he was the author of popular songs. He owned winning racehorses and was a top radio star. But eventually drinking and gambling cursed his life.

Then Billy Graham came in a citywide campaign to Los Angeles, California. Hearing him, Stuart Hamblen was so terribly convicted of sin that he tried to drown his feelings in drink and fled from the city. Often those who seem farthest from yielding to God are most strongly convicted and near the kingdom. Stuart returned to Los Angeles and, finally, on October 17, 1949, at 4:30 in the morning he was converted and became a Christian in Billy Graham's hotel room. Hollywood laughed and thought his conversion would not last. But he gave up his worldly broadcasts, sold his racehorses, and began to live for God. Soon God helped him write a song of encouragement that swept over America and began to be sung everywhere. It tells of God's forgiving power:

> *It is no secret what God can do,*
> *What He's done for others, He'll do for you.*
> *With arms wide open, He'll pardon you;*
> *It is no secret what God can do.*

At that same time in Hollywood, Harvey Fritz, a famous television actor, was brought to God. A year before, he had lined his family against a wall, threatening to kill them all. Fame and money had only made him unhappy and desperate. During the same revival in Los Angeles, Fritz was converted at about midnight as he knelt in the campaign tent after a regular service. He arose with a shining face and felt compelled to share his testimony. He opened his next television program with the song "Sweet Hour of Prayer" and then testified how Christ had forgiven his sins and changed his life. He lost his TV contract with its high pay, but he was supremely happy in Christ.

During the same revival campaign Jim Vaus was converted. He was drawn to the meetings by the story of the conversion of Stuart Hamblen and Harvey Fritz. Vaus had been a wiretapper, gambler, and henchman for a man famous in the crime world, but this man was in the penitentiary at that time. Vaus was the son of a minister and was himself a former theological student. God convicted and saved this wayward man, and he made public confession, paying over $15,000 in restitution to those he had wronged (see Ex. 22:3, 5–6, 12).

Such unusual and striking conversions amazed the whole city of Los Angeles so that the total attendance at the meetings reached 350,000. Over 6,000 people made decisions for Christ. This was a turning point in the work of Billy Graham; since then God has opened many doors for his ministry.

It is no secret what God can do. In the most hopeless cases, at the very time when a desperate soul seems most hopeless, he can yield to Christ when God's people really pray. It is time for each one of us to begin with a new faith and in holy desperation pray for the situations that have not changed despite our efforts and prayers. A delayed answer may only mean that Satan is fighting hard, for he fears the results of those efforts and prayers. Believe God and by faith claim the impossible from Him. It is no secret that no case is too hard for God to handle. And it is no secret what God can do when you pray.

Lord, help me believe that You will work a miracle.

Is Your Heart Ablaze?

The first New Testament revival began when God's fire from heaven fell upon the hearts of Jesus' disciples. They were already true children of God, but not until the Day of Pentecost were their hearts truly set ablaze. From that day to this, every mighty revival can be characterized in two ways—from God's standpoint revival is His divine visitation in Holy Spirit power, and from man's standpoint it is hearts set ablaze by the fire of the Holy Spirit. Whenever God the Holy Spirit visits the people of God, He sets their hearts ablaze. Whenever a child of God is filled with the Spirit of God, his heart is set ablaze. Is your heart ablaze?

Regardless of the condition of the hearts of others, your heart can be ablaze for God. Revival does not depend on your environment; revival depends on your own heart's relation to God. You can have a revival in your heart even though no one else around you does. Does it seem to you that there are few in your church who are yearning for a visitation from God? Is there almost no interest on the part of the local leaders of your church to pray for revival? Are sins of professing Christians hindering the witness of your church? These conditions may make revival more difficult, but they also make revival an absolute necessity. Such conditions, however, should in no way prevent you from having personal revival in your own heart.

Revival in your heart can be helped by fellowship with other people who are ablaze for God, but only in an indirect way. Revival fire is directly the fire of the Holy Spirit. This fire comes from God, not from other people. God will visit any prepared heart. It is a blessing to hear the testimonies of other people whose hearts have been set ablaze for God; it is a blessing to feel the power in the prayer of such revived Christians. But whether or not such a privilege is possible for you, God is still waiting to meet you. You can be ablaze for God in any environment.

The Holy Spirit is given to those who obey God (Acts 5:32), and you can obey God whether others do or not. The Holy Spirit is given to those who ask for His presence (Luke 11:13), and you can ask whether or not others ask. Those who are hungry and thirsty for God will be filled (Matt. 5:6), and you can hunger all you want to. If no one else is hungry, you can still reach out for more of God.

Oh, Christian friend, be encouraged. You can have as much of God's presence and power in your life as you desire. Hunger, ask, and obey, and you will surely receive. Your heart can feel the fire of God in the midst of the coldest surroundings. Your heart can flame for God in the midst of the darkest spiritual environment. You can have as much of God in your life as you truly hunger for. You can have revival fire regardless of what others do or have in their hearts.

Fire tends to die out, and often revival blessings in others seem to disappear in a disappointingly short time. Your heart will also tend to grow cold unless you constantly keep being refilled by new outpourings of God's Spirit upon you. But if you keep reaching out for God and if you keep obeying God, you can keep your heart ablaze for Him. Revival fire need never die. The glory cloud and fire of God's presence remained with the Israelites during the forty years of their desert wanderings. The Shekinah fire and glory of God among Israel remained in the temple in the Most Holy Place for centuries. You too can keep God's fire burning on the altar of your soul. You too can keep a heart so ablaze for God that your life is constantly marked by His presence and glory. The fire in the hearts of those about you may flame up for a while and then die down, but this need not be your experience. You can keep God's fire and glory constantly in your soul if you are willing to pay the price of constant surrender, constant obedience, and constant seeking more of God.

One fire kindles another. Every heart must get its fire from God the Holy Spirit. But as your heart is victoriously aglow for God, as your love burns at white-hot intensity, as your faith flames out into the darkness, as you keep your heart's altar covered with the Shekinah fire and glory of God, others among you are going to get hungry for revival too and will begin to reach out for God in a new way.

Get the fire, guard the holy fire, and scatter this holy fire far and wide. You can be ablaze for God today and every day if you are willing to pay the price. You can have as much of God in your life as you really want. Ask, and it shall be given.

Lord, set me ablaze and keep me ablaze!

 God Loves You

God has had plans for you personally from all eternity. Before you or your parents were born, before Christ was born, even before there was an earth and a universe, God has been planning for you. Billions of people have lived and died, and the human population of earth is rapidly increasing. God knows the details of every one of these lives, but He also has a special plan and purpose for you. We could not believe this to be true if God had not made it very clear in His Word.

What a blessed reality this is! God's very nature is perfect love. There is infinite and constant perfect love within the blessed Trinity. God the Father, God the Son, and God the Holy Spirit find their greatest fellowship and their greatest joy in one another. The three persons of the Trinity are able to give themselves infinitely to each other and feel the infinite loving response from each other. They have no deeper and more holy satisfaction and joy than from this fellowship with one another.

Furthermore, God is able to lavish constantly and marvelously His perfect love on the myriads of His holy angels. Continually, instantly, and joyfully, they do His perfect will. Day and night they worship Him in loving adoration. His wonderful Being is their constant meditation and joy. His service is their constant blessed privilege. They lovingly adore Him, and they rejoice to please Him and bring constant holy satisfaction to His infinitely loving heart.

Then how could God possibly find such delightful additional joy or blessedness in loving you and me? It would almost seem His love of us would be to Him a useless waste. Our greatest love seems so unresponsive and worthless in comparison to the love He already has within the Trinity and among the angels that our love must always seem weak, imperfect, and small. Although He always remembers us, we sometimes forget Him. His love for us and His hunger for our love never changes, yet our love for Him often cools.

We so often neglect Him for the lesser things of this world, and we so quickly forget our first love to Him that He cannot but be constantly disappointed in us. The more He lavishes His infinite love on us, the more disappointing our feeble responses must seem to Him! The more He hungers for us, the more our hunger and love for Him must seem painfully lacking! Oh, my fellow Christian, how can God love us so?

Surely you have never understood how amazing it is that God even takes notice of you! But that is not all. He loves you. He loves you with the same infinite love with which He loves His Son and with which God the Son loves Him. Can this possibly be? Can we believe this to be true? We must! Listen to the words of Jesus: "As the Father has loved me, so have I loved you" (John 15:9). "You . . . have loved them even as you have loved me" (17:23). ". . . That the love you have for me may be in them and that I myself may be in them" (v. 26).

God the Father loves you with the same infinite, perfect, constant, and eternal love with which He loves His Son. God the Father loved the Son before the creation of the world (John 17:24) and God loved you from before the creation of the world. "In His love He chose us—actually picked us out for Himself as His own—in Christ before the foundation of the world" (Eph. 1:4 AMPLIFIED).

God has the same tender interest and perfect concern in every detail of your life as He had in the earthly life of Jesus. The Father delights in your every prayer, in your every loving thought, and in your every remembrance of Him, just as He delights in every loving response of Jesus Christ to His infinite love. God the Father is hungry for you with the same yearning love with which He yearns for His only Son.

My Christian brothers and sisters, fall on your faces in reverence before this holy mystery. God loves you as He loves His only Son. How can you be so casual and so indifferent in your love to Him? God loves you every moment, day and night, when you are awake and when you are asleep, when you are praying and when you are working, when you are well and when you are ill, when you are joyfully serving Him and even when you are disappointing Him.

You have often failed Him, but He has never ceased to love you. You have often forgotten Him, but never for one moment has He forgotten you. You have often grieved Him, but He has loved you no less. His love for you has only been made more painfully intense. Never in your most lonely moment are you outside His love. Every time you begin to lift your heart in prayer His heart is thrilled that you are again looking to Him, and His wonderful and infinite heart is reaching out in perfect, yearning love for you.

I am sure you have never realized how much God loves you. It would be absolutely impossible for you ever, ever to fully realize it. His love for you is so personal, so infinite, so wonderful, so considerate. He longs for you. He plans for you. He cares for you. He rejoices in you. He waits for you. He goes before you. He follows you. He surrounds you. He is too wonderful for human description. All that I can say to you is that God loves you—God, God! Think of it! Pause in reverent wonder and amazement. GOD loves you!

Come and rest in this wonderful assurance! Come and share with Him all your heart's desire. He is your Father, and He loves you. He is just waiting to hear your voice in prayer. Why should you worry when God loves you so greatly? Let your heart sing for joy. But, pause and think—what a solemn call this is for your loving response for the rest of your life. I say it in hushed tones, God loves you; fall on your knees, then, and worship and love and obey Him. My brother, my sister, GOD loves you!

∞

Father, help me respond constantly to Your love.

A Great Year for You

God longs for this to be a great year of personal revival for you! God desires this to be the greatest year you have ever known. Maybe you have prayed often for the salvation of friends, for increased blessing on your work, and for a new anointing on your life. Perhaps many of these prayers have not had the full answer you have been longing for. Do not be discouraged; take a new grip on God in simple living faith. God wants this to be the year of answered prayer that you have been longing for. From God's standpoint there is not the slightest reason why this should not be a miracle year for you!

There is strong scriptural proof that God wants your present spiritual life to be the best you have ever known, your present prayer life to be the most fruitful you have ever known, your present love for Christ to be the deepest and strongest you have ever known, and your present daily experience to be the most victorious you have ever known. God wants your life to be richer, fuller, deeper, more blessed, and more anointed every passing year.

God always plans that your future be better than your past. This year is full of blessings that God is longing to bestow on you personally. Unworthy as you have been and still are, God loves you with an exceedingly deep and tender love. He is ready to do as much for your personal spiritual life as He has ever done for the life of anyone else. Believe in His deeply personal love, His power, and His all-sufficiency for you.

There is scriptural proof that God is longing to work through you. Whoever you are, wherever you are, God wants you to be His salt, His light, His seed, His witness, His ambassador, His co-laborer. God wants to work through you more now than He has ever been able to do in the past. The Holy Spirit has been promised to cleanse and empower you so that you may be God's co-laborer.

Humanly speaking, you are utterly unworthy, incapable, and completely insufficient. Humanly speaking, you cannot expect to be a co-laborer with God. Even if God condescended to choose you for His servant, how could you become His co-laborer? God knew it was utterly impossible for you to do this in your own strength, your own wisdom, and your own nature. This is why He promises you the Holy Spirit. All you need you can find in Him.

All the radiance, wisdom, and power you need is promised in Him. The fruits you need are fruits of the Spirit, the guidance you need is guidance of the Spirit, the wisdom you need is wisdom of the Spirit, the power you need is the power of the Spirit. All you need is promised to you through God's Holy Spirit. Do you know Him? Do you know His mighty cleansing, mighty empowering, mighty indwelling? You can be God's co-worker, God's instrument of revival if the Holy Spirit cleanses, fills, and indwells you completely.

God has chosen that revival be a work in which we work together with Him. We cannot bring revival by our own efforts, but God has chosen not to send revival without our cooperation. When God desires to work mightily, He puts deep desires in the hearts of His people, He draws His people to pray more earnestly, and He calls them to new and fuller steps of obedience.

Is not God working in your life now? Do you not believe that God desires new blessings on His church and an ingathering of new believers? Has not God made every provision? Has He not placed His hand upon your own life, even though you may feel unworthy of His love? Believe in Him and obey Him. Expect great things; attempt great things in His power. God is depending on you to help bring about a revival this year.

Lord, make this whole year all You desire it to be.

Your Greatest Need

12

You are constantly in danger of forgetting how utterly dependent you are on the Holy Spirit. It is so easy to forget what a divine, all-comprehensive, and mighty ministry the Holy Spirit desires to have in you and through you. You cannot live for God or work for God without the enabling grace of God as ministered to you through the Spirit.

Yet there is constant danger, even if you are a committed, spiritual Christian, that you will begin to rely on past experiences of the working of God's grace. There may be the constant temptation to rely too exclusively on essentially human resources, such as the assistance of fellow Christians or Christian organizations, or on your own methods and efforts. There is even the danger of relying on your own Christian experience or maturity. Again and again you need to be reminded of your need of the Holy Spirit.

The Holy Spirit is so self-effacing in His ministry that you will often fail to realize the strength and extent of His working. The Holy Spirit does, indeed, perform from time to time such miracles of grace and power that we are amazed, convicted, or overwhelmed by the sense of God's presence and working; but, contrary to the opinions of many, the major ministry of the Spirit is not in the realm of the amazing and the spectacular. The constant ministry of infilling, cleansing, anointing, empowering, guiding, and making fruitful is of even greater importance. Without this ministry you cannot live the life of the Spirit. If you limit this ministry by the attitudes of your heart and by inadequate responses, you remain weak, ineffectual, and largely fruitless. Pray for, welcome, and submit yourself to the gracious ministry of the Holy Spirit.

You need the Holy Spirit to enable you to live a life of victory and radiance. The Spirit-filled life is possible only as He fills you. Only then can He manifest His power within you. Victory over temptation and the strength to be what you ought to be will be natural and normal to you only if He is Lord of your life completely. The lordship of the Spirit is very real and is always manifest in the transformation and empowering of your life. You need this indwelling of the mighty God, this transforming lordship, and this inner endowment.

You need the Holy Spirit for the effective fulfillment of your ministry. God requires some ministry from those who have been born again. Each of us is called to be a witness. The Holy Spirit is the Great Witness. You will not witness effectively by your life apart from His indwelling witness. You will not witness effectively by your lips without the Spirit's anointing. Your Spirit-filled life as a child of God can be so Christlike, so beautiful, so holy, and so power filled that others will recognize that you belong to Christ. The infilling fullness of the Holy Spirit must make a distinguishing difference in you as a child of God.

Every Christian must witness with his lips; yet even without any verbal witness it is impossible for a Spirit-filled life to be hidden. If you can live and work with others without their realizing that you are different in your inner nature and that you belong to Christ, are you really filled with the Spirit? The Great Witness cannot be hidden when you are filled with Him.

Some will be attracted to the Christian faith through you (even though they may deny this). Others may be angered because they feel convicted by your holy, happy, Spirit-filled life, but they cannot help being impressed by it. The tragedy is that many Christians are not effectively witnessing in this way. Obviously they lack the full ministry of the Spirit. The church and the world are waiting for you and me to be really filled by the transforming Spirit of God.

The prayer ministry that God expects from us is also impossible apart from the ministry of the Spirit. Have you realized that on the Judgment Day you will be asked to give an account of how you prayed for others and how much you prayed for others? Be sure of this: You can fulfill this ministry of prayer in the way God desires only when you are under the complete lordship of the Holy Spirit.

You need the Spirit to guide you so that you will know for whom to pray. You cannot pray for everyone all the time. Each day you will be selective in your prayers, for the Spirit of God knows who most needs your prayer at any given time. Even when you use prayer lists, the Spirit may draw your attention to a particular name at the time when that person needs special prayer. You need the Spirit to guide you when to pray. You may be engaged in other activities, but the Spirit can guide you at the exact time your prayer is needed if you are Spirit-filled and sensitive to His leading.

You need the Holy Spirit to deepen your love and earnestness so that you can pray with real concern and at times engage in what the Bible calls "wrestling" in prayer, or prayer warfare. You need the Holy Spirit to give birth to true faith within you so that you can pray the kind of prayer that appropriates God's promise and prevails until God gives the victory.

There isn't a day that goes by without your need of the Holy Spirit to guide you in what you say, in what you pray, and in what you do. There isn't a day that passes without your need of the transforming grace, radiant beauty, and mighty power of the Holy Spirit. You and I need Him above all other needs.

We need Him in our personal lives, we need Him in our ministry, we need Him in our homes, in our churches, and in all our organizations. He is the One we need above all else.

Ask, and He will be given to you (Luke 11:13). Welcome Him, and He will work fully and freely within you. Abandon yourself to Him, and He will take the entire responsibility for your life. Obey Him, and He will anoint and use you. He has been promised to you by God the Son; He has been given to you by God the Father. Oh, let Him come in, let Him fill you completely, let Him be your all. He is God the Spirit. He longs to meet all your needs. He is your greatest need.

Come, Holy Spirit, fill me more and more.

Life Is Too Brief to Waste

You have one brief moment of life, with an unending eternity following it. You have only one brief lifetime, and it is going by faster than you realize; so invest your life wisely for eternity. Part of your life is already past—perhaps most of it. The only remaining moment of life that you can be sure of is the present moment. You can also be sure of an eternity of reaping. How much of your life and how many of your hours have already been invested for eternity?

You can waste much of your life and lose it, or you can invest it in faithful service and reap an eternal harvest of joy. Christ warns you that if you save your life for yourself you will lose it (Matt. 16:25). The only way to save your life eternally is to invest it: Give it to God and give it for others. True, you owe your life to God, but if you give it joyously and freely back to Him, He will count it as your investment, and He will reward you infinitely and eternally.

What a privilege! You can invest prayer in God's church around the world. You can invest love and prayer in the lives of hundreds and thousands of people. You can strengthen the leaders of Christ's cause by standing beside them in prayer. You can wipe the fevered brow of sufferers by loving prayer. You can bring comfort

to Christians living in countries where persecution is severe—
sometimes unimaginably severe. You can love and give and pray.

At the Judgment, Jesus will say to some, "I was hungry and
you gave me nothing to eat, I was thirsty and you gave me nothing to drink, I was a stranger and you did not invite me in, I needed clothes and you did not clothe me, I was sick and in prison and
you did not look after me" (Matt. 25:42–43). If we answer, "When,
Lord? When?" we will probably find that we failed Jesus most often
in our prayer life. He may remind us that often we did not even pray
once a day for more than one or two specific gospel ministries. We
were not really persistent in praying for our needy cities, for the
criminals, for the spiritually starving and lost. We rarely shed a tear
for the mission fields and did not consistently carry a real prayer
burden for any of them. You may be surprised to know—when
Christ shows you—how little you loved, cared, and prayed for
Christ's kingdom, and how little you sacrificed for Him.

How much revival could you reasonably expect from the prayer
you invested in your community, your nation, your world? How
many times has Christ been disappointed at the lack of time you
really invested in prayer? What explanation will you give Him
when He tells you that you lived as if you were not going to be judged
for how you lived your life after you were saved (1 Cor. 3:10–15)?

Don't waste your time on trivial things. How much of the
time you spend on reading newspapers and listening to the radio
and watching television will be an eternal loss for you? How much
time you have spent on your hobbies will have no value at the Judgment? Is much of your conversational time spent merely repeating
what you and others already know? Could what you say just as
well have been left unsaid?

Why not spend that same amount of time with friends praying together for the leaders of this country, for the conversion of
some of your friends, for God to raise up new leaders from among
the youth about you? Think of it! How many times could you and
your friends have easily invested five minutes, fifteen minutes, even
a half hour in prayer time and have attained God's reward for all
eternity? Oh, life is too brief to waste!

You can weep as you pray for the orphans; you can love as you pray for little children who don't know Jesus. You can take new converts into your loving arms of prayer; you can strengthen your pastors and leaders as you pray for them. You can lift the loads from the hearts of the Christians in lands where they are persecuted today. You can help and encourage small groups of Christians in hostile environments by praying for them. You can pray for a spiritual harvest in Russia and China. How often do you intercede mightily for Islamic lands? Or do you not love their people enough to pray for them? How many places around the world, how many world leaders, how many of the government leaders are on your daily prayer list? How many unsaved people around you do you pray for by name each day? If you invest your life in others around the world, then in eternity they will greet you and thank you over and over.

If you are too spiritually asleep and lazy, you can forget your prayer life, and wait to weep until you stand before Christ's judgment throne. Will your life have been largely wasted? Will you have wasted hours and hours and hours in carelessness while the world was heading toward hell?

Pray as you travel, praise as you go about your duties, love God and others as you think of them. Think of it! By investing minutes daily, which added together will become hours and days, you are investing your life for eternity. True love is never lost; true prayer will never die. Give your all, sow your time, invest your life for eternity. LIFE IS TOO BRIEF AND PRECIOUS TO WASTE.

∞

O Lord, help me to use today to the full.

∞

Life Is Too Brief to Waste

We march across the stage of time
From dawn to set of sun;
We catch a glimpse of things sublime,
Of work that must be done.
We plan for all that we would do

And for our calling train.
We hope to see our vision through
And real success attain.

How many finish earth's brief way
Just when their work's begun,
And oft the noontide of life's day
For them means setting sun.
How often in the prime of life
Man puts his work aside,
And leaving children, home, and wife
Confronts life's ebbing tide.

How many drop a cherished plan
Just when success seems near,
When suddenly they find that man
Is but a mortal here.
How many cherish long a goal
Which they would fain attain,
But that on which man sets his soul
How oft he fails to gain!

Life is too brief to lose one day
E'en though your life prove long.
You pass but once along life's way,
You sing but once life's song.
You have but one life to invest
For ages without end.
You dare not fail to do your best—
But one life do you spend.

God's daily guidance must be sought
Or moments may be lost;
Our plans must all to Him be brought
And we must count the cost.
God help us His own will to choose
And His own work to haste.
We dare not life's brief moment lose—
Life is too brief to waste.

Wesley L. Duewel

You Can Bless the World 14

Have you realized that God wants you to bless the world by your prayer life? Paul asks you to make your priority blessing people by your prayer. "I urge, then, first of all, that requests, prayers, intercession and thanksgiving be made for everyone" (1 Tim. 2:1). For everyone? Yes. One translation of this verse words it this way: "regularly for all men." Another has "for all mankind."

God desires that each day your prayer life include prayers to bless others. The paraphrase of *The Living Bible* for this verse states, "Here are my directions: Pray much for others; plead for God's mercy upon them; give thanks for all he is going to do for them." Do you have that kind of a daily intercessory prayer life for others? Have you discovered the joy there is in praying for others? Do you realize what a joy it is for Jesus when He prays for you and all of His children each day?

Who should be on your priority prayer list? For whom should you pray daily? Paul explains in the next verse, "Pray in this way for kings and all others who are in authority over us, or are in places of high responsibility" (LB). He emphasizes two things and therefore clarifies God's will for our prayer lives.

First, God holds us responsible for praying every day for government leaders. God wants us to make a difference in our government by our prayer life. Surely every government needs much prayer. What a difference would occur in the world and in our own government if every Christian prayed fervently every day for his or her government and the leaders of the government. You have no right to criticize your government if you are not actively praying for it. God will hold you accountable for criticizing without praying when you stand before His judgment throne.

Not only are you to pray about the needs of your nation—the sins, the decisions, the policies, and the actions of the government—but you should also pray for the individuals who lead your government. Which individuals? For "all those in authority over us." Who are these? For me, as an American, that involves a number of people. What government leaders' names should be on your daily prayer list?

Your list should probably include your president and vice president, your senators, your representative in Congress, your governor, and your mayor. Would it not include the names of all the Supreme Court justices? Do you need to include the president's cabinet members? The acts and decisions of these people affect our whole nation. Every one of them needs prayer. It is not enough just to ask God to bless all those in authority. We need to pray for them personally. If you were in their position, wouldn't you want people to pray for you? No one knows enough to always make the right decisions.

A major sin of many Christians is their failure to pray for their government and its leaders. Sin? Yes! It is a sin when you fail to pray for those for whom God told you to pray (see 1 Sam. 12:23).

But, you reply, it would take time to pray for all our leaders. Of course it does. God expects you to take time in prayer. You are probably not spending as much time in prayer as He longs for you to do. The responsibility of intercession is a major responsibility that God requires of all Christians. Don't arrive in heaven having failed to spend adequate time in prayer and having failed to pray for the people God expects you to include in your daily intercession.

But there is more in 1 Timothy 2:2. Note that *kings* is plural. You have only one king or one president. True! But God expects your prayer to include more than the leaders of your own nation. God wants each of us to be world Christians. God so loved the world that He gave. He wants you to love the world enough to pray.

You cannot pray every day for everybody in the whole world. But you can make great differences in many parts of the world by faithful daily prayer. Following are some suggestions for your prayer time and your prayer list. Perhaps you are already praying for all these things. But if you are not, let me suggest them to you.

1. *Ask God to give you a special concern for at least two or three other nations,* and then pray for these nations every day. You may want to pray for other nations also, but at least take two or three nations upon your heart as your daily personal responsibility.

2. *Pray daily for God to bless all missionary evangelism*—personal evangelism, public evangelism, witness teams, missionary radio and TV, and evangelistic literature—in other parts of the world.

3. *Pray daily for the training of Christian leaders* in Bible schools, colleges, and seminaries in the various nations around the world.

4. *Pray daily for the needy areas currently in the news.* Pray for those places where there is war. Pray for God to restrain the evil and alleviate the suffering and to bring peace. Pray for places where there have been needs because of earthquakes, famine, rioting, or other calamities.

5. *Pray for Christians who are being oppressed or opposed for Christ's sake.* The Bible tells us we are to stand beside them and uphold them (Heb. 10:33; Rom. 12:15). At least we can do that by prayer. Many Christians in Communist or Muslim nations urgently need you to stand beside them in prayer.

6. *Pray for world revival and world harvest.* Each of us should have a prayer burden for the unsaved and, of course, we should pray for the unsaved in our own community—those whom God has specially placed on our hearts. You will want to have a number of such names on your daily prayer list. But that is not enough. You need to yearn with Jesus for the unsaved people throughout the world whom He wants to be brought into His fold (John 10:16).

7. *Pray for the personal spiritual health and financial needs of missionaries, pastors, evangelists, and other Christian workers* in various parts of the world. I hope you have a number of Christian workers on your daily prayer list. You can convey your love to them by prayer. You can actually strengthen them by your prayer.

You can bless the world. As Jesus wept over Jerusalem, you can carry a prayer burden and at times fast and weep for one or more cities or other places in the world. You can learn to love with the love that Jesus had. In my childhood I heard my mother day after day weep during family prayer as she prayed for the people in China and in India. She loved them with a Christlike love. She was a priest of God for those nations.

I want you to be a priest of God. I want you to have great reward when you get to heaven because you have been faithful in your prayer life. I want you to bless the world, ask Him to bless the nations, and bring daily joy to Jesus by your intercession. Oh, how great your reward will be if faithfully, day after day, you join with Jesus in asking that the nations will be His inheritance (Ps. 2:8)!

Lord, bless the world through my prayer each day.

Wait, Because . . .

If you have wondered why your prayer has not been answered yet, "Wait" is God's answer to you. You have been so certain that your prayer was in the will of God. God Himself has been leading you. He has kept His hand on your life. He has blessed you. But you have one question that still remains; one prayer that is still unanswered. Why? Why?

Habakkuk asked such a question, and the Lord answered him. "Then the Lord replied: 'Write down the revelation and make it plain on tablets so that a herald may run with it. For the revelation awaits an appointed time; it speaks of the end and will not prove false. Though it linger, wait for it; it will certainly come and will not delay'" (Hab. 2:2–3).

Wait, God says to you. Wait, because God is working out His highest purpose. Wait, because God knows best and does best. Here He gives you four reasons why you can wait and rejoice. Wait with confident assurance; wait for God's purpose; wait, because. . . .

First: Wait, because God has appointed His time. God plans His actions perfectly. He not only has perfect knowledge of all present circumstances, but He also foresees all that is in the future. God never acts before the best time; He never acts too late. God has a glorious and perfect strategy. He answers prayer when it will bring the greatest good to you and the greatest glory to Him. He knows when His miracle will be exactly appropriate. His love has set His time. Wait, because God's time is coming.

Second: Wait, because the answer to your prayer is hastening. God is sovereign over all the circumstances of your life. He has been preparing you for the answer to your prayer. He has also been preparing other lives and other circumstances for this very thing. He is making all things work together for your good (Rom. 8:28). His preparation is already well advanced. His holy angels are assisting in the preparation and are ministering for your good. The unseen prayers of unknown saints of God are joining in the prayers of Christ and the Holy Spirit on your behalf.

All the resources of God are available for meeting your need. God will not permit anyone or anything to divert Him from His purpose. He has begun the preparation for the answer to your prayer, and He will complete what He has begun. Wait, because the answer to your prayer is nearer than ever before. Wait, because all things are working together for your good.

Third: Wait, because God will be true. God cannot lie, and the vision He gives to you will be fulfilled. All else may change, but God's purpose is unchangeable. His love for you will never change; His knowledge of your situations will always be complete. His power will never be less than almighty. God's Word will stand forever; His promise to you can never, never fail. Wait, because God will do exactly as He has promised.

Fourth: Wait, because God will not delay His answer. The only delays are those necessary to allow you time for better preparation of your own heart and life, or to allow for all the circumstances to fit together for God's greater glory and your own greater good. God never waits without a wonderful purpose. There are no fatal delays in God's working—there are only opportunities for God to work His greatest miracles. God will delay only when that very delay is a crucial part of His total plan for you. Wait, because God waits only so that He may be more gracious to you (Isa. 30:18).

Be encouraged, trust and praise God for the answer that is sure to come. God can never forget you or His good purpose for you. His time for your prayer to be answered is appointed; His plan is established. His answer is hastening on its way. He will not change; He will not be slow to answer you. God's miracle is on the way; tomorrow you will see it if you keep obeying God. "Consecrate yourselves, for tomorrow the Lord will do amazing things among you" (Josh. 3:5).

Lord, teach me to rejoice as I wait.

Your Wonderful Father 16

You have a wonderful Father in heaven and a wonderful family of His children on earth. Both your heavenly Father and, ideally, your brothers and sisters in God's family love you so much that they constantly enter into all your life by caring for you and helping you. From the time you are born into God's family through a new birth you are never without a wonderful Father and a wonderful family. You are never unloved, you are never forgotten, you are never alone, and you are never without a Helper.

1. *You have a wonderful Father.* As a true Christian you have been born of God. He is not merely your wonderful God but also your wonderful Father. One of the deepest and most wonderful lessons of the Bible is that God is our Father. We do not truly pray unless we approach God as our Father. True, He is our Creator, our almighty God, and our sovereign King. But above all, He is the Father of His children. He is almighty and eternal; He is the almighty and eternal Father. A major purpose of Christ's coming was to reveal to us the fatherhood of God.

God's most important, most amazing, and most blessed relationship to the Christian is that of Father. Whatever else you have or do not have, you always have a Father. You are never helpless and alone, you are never without One who cares. You have known human fatherhood; all the best in human fatherhood is but a shadow when compared with the wonderful fatherhood of God. Unfortunately, many of us have not had an ideal human father. God can mean all that and infinitely more to you compared with all that the best earthly father can mean to his most loved child.

2. *Your Father bears your burdens.* From the moment you are born into God's family, you have a heavenly Father who will always love you and care for you. It is natural for children to bring all their cares and worries to their father and mother and make them the parents' responsibility. This is exactly what God wants you to do with Him. "Casting the whole of your care—all your anxieties, all your worries, all your concerns, once and for all—on Him, for He cares for you affectionately, *and* cares about you watchfully" (1 Peter 5:7, AMPLIFIED). David adds, "Commit your way to the Lord" (Ps. 37:5). You can commit the whole of your life, your pathway, with all its responsibility, cares, and burdens to God your Father. This should be done in a full surrender once and for all. It is also scriptural and blessed to go on committing daily all your anxieties, cares, and burdens to Him. "So we say with confidence, 'The Lord is my helper; I will not be afraid'" (Heb. 13:6).

3. *Your Father knows all your need.* "Your heavenly Father knows" (Matt. 6:32). This is Christ's wonderful assurance to us. The Father knows the birds of the air and cares for them; He knows the flowers of the field and cares for them. He knows everything about your life—even the number of the hairs on your head (Matt. 10:30).

You cannot inform Him about anything new; you cannot explain anything He does not already know and understand. Yet He wants you to come freely and share all the details with Him. He knows why your burdens are particularly heavy. He knows all the circumstances surrounding you today, all the obstacles facing you, and all the discouraging things that have happened to you. He knows. How wonderful, how comforting! He cares for you. He has given you His promises. He knows every single detail of your life. He sees. He knows. He understands.

Cast your burdens on your wonderful Father. He knows all about you and your burdens. He feels all that your heart feels. He sympathizes and understands. He will not leave you or forsake you. He wants to comfort you more than your mother or father could ever do. He wants to be all you need. You have carried your burdens too long already; just throw them off your shoulders and roll them onto His shoulders. "Cast your cares on the Lord and He will sustain you" (Ps. 55:22). He will take all the responsibility for your care. Give the Lord your burden and leave it in His great hands.

Lord, thank You for Your loving care. I cast all my burdens on You.

Your Burden-bearing Family

Your Christian brothers and sisters bear your burdens. As certainly as God your Father bears your burdens, your brothers and sisters in Christ also bear your burdens. God knows our burdens are often too much for us to bear alone, so He lets our wonderful family share these burdens with us.

All of God's world is governed by law—the expression of His will. Just as there are laws of seedtime and harvest, of day and night, so there are also spiritual laws of faith and prayer. One spiritual law is the law of bearing others' burdens. This is called the law of Christ (Gal. 6:2). As soon as your burden becomes too heavy for you, God places your burden on other Christian brothers and sisters. Immediately someone somewhere begins to feel your load and will share it with you. That person may never have met you or heard of you, but God will place your prayer concern on his or her heart. God uses the faithful prayers of others to strengthen and encourage you.

While you are on earth, you probably will never know who shared a specific burden with you. One of the joys of eternity will be finding out those whom God has used to bless and help you. It will be a holy joy to them as well as to you when they discover whose burden it was they helped share. You will find on that great day that thousands of hands have upheld your life—hands of love from all over the world, hands of love from all races and languages—unseen holy hands upholding you and sharing your burdens. How wonderful, and how blessedly true!

I have just returned from three months of speaking engagements in eight countries. During that time I had up to six, seven, and eight engagements on my busiest days. Throughout this whole trip the sense of being upheld by the prayers of others was so blessedly real. One night I had a high fever, my body ached, my head ached, there was much nausea. But at about ten o'clock that night as I traveled alone on the train, feeling at the end of myself, I suddenly felt as if a human hand took a cool, wet washcloth and wiped my fevered brow. Instantly my aches and pains were gone, and I was completely well. I knew someone had prayed for me. Later I received a letter stating that at 9:55 that very night God had put a prayer burden for me on a Christian friend.

Reaching another country weeks later, a woman came to me at the close of the service and said that from the night I had left India God had been waking her early each morning to pray for me. In different countries I had the joy of meeting readers of *Revival* (the magazine I had been editing from India; we published it in twelve languages for some years). They told how they had all been blessed by *Revival* magazine and had been praying for me. I found that for seventeen, eighteen, nineteen, and even twenty years they had been praying for me.

One night in Australia an announced place of meeting was suddenly changed from the city church to a remote rural church. After the service that night an aged saint called me to her seat and said, "For years I have been praying for you. I have been praying for you at four o'clock in the morning. . . . For several years I have prayed God to send you to Australia and to this church." Then I realized the reason why my schedule had been changed so suddenly. God had rearranged my schedule so I could meet her in answer to her years of prayer. How humbled one feels to learn of such faithful prayer!

Eternity will reveal the many thousands of people upholding you and me in prayer today. Others are bearing our burdens.

Not only so, but all of God's angelic host are available to help us in our need. Are they not all ministering spirits sent to serve us (Heb. 1:14)? Even when we are unaware, angelic hands will aid us and lift our load whenever God sends them to us. They are members of God's greater family; they are ready even now to help us.

Thank God, we also have our Elder Brother, Jesus Christ, who is able "to understand *and* sympathize *and* have a shared feeling with our weaknesses *and* infirmities *and* liability to the assaults of temptation" (Heb. 4:15, AMPLIFIED). He is the most wonderful Burden-Sharer of all! Surely He bears our griefs and carries our sorrows even today (Isa. 53:4). He is the same yesterday, today, and forever (Heb. 13:8). He weeps with you today as much as He wept with Mary and Martha. He shares instantly every burden you bear. "Cast all your anxiety on him because he cares for you" (1 Peter 5:7).

Christian, you have a wonderful family, and all your family is sharing and helping bear your burdens. Take new courage, dry your tears, lift up your head! Your heavenly Father knows and cares. Your brothers and sisters in other places may even now be sharing an unseen prayer burden for you. Angelic hosts are ministering to you even though you don't see them. And Jesus Christ, your great High Priest, your Elder Brother, is sharing every part of your burden. You are not alone. You are part of God's wonderful loving, burden-sharing family. And they are caring for you!

Lord, thank You that Your wonderful family is also mine.

God's Power Is for You!

God wants you to understand more fully and to appropriate more adequately His mighty power. God is a personal Being of infinite power. Being a person, He exercises His power according to wisdom and love. As the Father of a spiritual family, He desires to use His power in behalf of His family. You, His very own child, have a spiritual inheritance that includes "his incomparably great power" (Eph. 1:18–19).

Creation manifests the infinitude of His power. Providence demonstrates how God can wisely use that power to frustrate all His enemies, help you, and work in all things for your good (Rom. 8:28). The Cross demonstrates His infinite love. Christ's resurrection demonstrates the glory of the power that is available to you. His resurrection power is God's power available to you now— available for glorious victory in your own life and for a miracle by which He can be glorified—through your faith. God often glorifies Himself through His supernatural power in spite of our unbelief, but the Bible specifically declares that "his incomparably great power [is] for us who believe" (Eph. 1:19). God's power is specially available to a man or woman of faith. Have you been believing Him for that power?

The Holy Spirit is the Spirit of power, and when He fills you, you are clothed with God's power. You are clothed with power, first of all, to enable you to live the supernatural life of victory to which God calls you. It is also given to enable you to more adequately demonstrate God's glory to an unbelieving, needy world. You need power to pray effectively and get God-glorifying answers to your prayers. You need power to radiate positive goodness and holiness, power to witness forcefully by your life and by your lips. How much have you appropriated the Holy Spirit in the fullness of His purity and power in your personal life? Are you truly clothed with power as Christ promised (Luke 24:49)? If not, why not? If not now, when?

God's Word is a word of power. It has convicting power, converting power, cleansing power. It can transform your life, your home, and the most difficult situations you may face. It has power in your personal devotions and in all forms of intercessory prayer and prayer warfare. God's Word is the sword of the Spirit in every spiritual conflict that you may engage in.

The same power that spoke worlds into existence and preserves all material creation to this day (Heb. 1:3) is the word of power that we see when Christ rebuked the winds and the waves, gave sight to the blind, rebuked fevers and diseases even miles away, and raised the dead to life. How little have we appropriated and used God's powerful Word! How much God wants this powerful Word to richly indwell us!

The very name of Christ has supernatural power. This statement does not indicate superstitious belief in magic. Christ's name is all-powerful because it expresses His infinite Being and all-glorious nature. It is the name exalted high above all, the only name by which we may be saved. It is the name that gives us strength in believing; it is the name that grants authority to our prayer. It is the name that Satan hates, and from which demons flee. Just this week I saw evil spirits flee a fettered person because of the power of Jesus' name. The blood of Christ has power to make anyone clean.

Servant of Christ, you have been promised God's mighty power. Is it yours today? Is the Holy Spirit indwelling you and giving you power and constant victory over sin, strength in spiritual battle, and radiance in your daily walk? You also may know the "hope to which he has called you, the riches of his glorious inheritance in the saints, and his incomparably great power for us who believe" (Eph. 1:18–19). Make all these wonderful gifts your own today.

My primary concern is not to make you hungry to perform supernatural miracles in spectacular, unnecessary ways. Praise God, He can still heal and deliver us from storm or danger. But my plea is for you to know the fullness of His power in victorious living; in prevailing, situation-changing intercession; and in fruitful evangelism, even in the most difficult situations.

We need God's power in practical and God-glorifying ways in our living, in our churches, and on our mission fields. Some of these needs, like the opening up of the Muslim world, are so massive that mighty, prevailing prayer by all of us is called for. God's power must be shown in the daily normal living, praying, and serving in "us who believe." Let us pray and believe in God's grace, holiness, and love so that His resurrection power may be demonstrated in each of us—in our close walk with God and in God-glorifying mighty answers to our prayers.

❧

Lord, seal my life with Your power.

Forget Those Things

It is time to forget many things (Phil. 3:13–15). There are things you have remembered too long and too well. It is always the right time to forget many things if you are to make spiritual progress, but it is particularly important to make the beginning of a new period of your life a time to forget some things forever. A new day of faith and power will begin for you when you learn to forget those things. What things? The things the Holy Spirit will place His finger on just now, if you ask Him to.

You may be too conscious of your own insufficiency. You may know that you are not adequate for the task before you. You know how many things have appeared to be too difficult for you. You may have felt overwhelmed by them. You may be tortured at times by your own inability to do all that is expected of you.

You may be so conscious of your own weakness, your inabilities, and your past failures that it is almost impossible to have the faith you need for your task. Your mind has often been filled with doubt. You have worried. But God knew all about this when He called you. God has brought you to the place you are today because He has a perfect plan for you and He wants to carry out His purpose for you.

Now—forget your weakness and your inabilities. Forget your failures. Leave them all with God. He knew all about you when He chose you for His purpose. He wants to supply what you lack. Forget those things that have caused you to worry. They are robbing you of your peace and trust. They are robbing you of your joy.

Look to God. He wants to do His miracle in your tomorrow. He cannot work through you when you rely on your own strength. But in your weakness He can show His power. Out of your inabilities He can work His miracles. Trust God and give Him all the glory.

You have also remembered the failures of some of your friends for too long. You have remembered some of their actions because they hurt you. It seemed to you that these actions were deliberately done. How could your friends be so inconsiderate? Why? Why . . . ? Yes, you have been remembering them too often and too long already. Forget those things.

These hurts have filled your life with tension and strain. They have weighted you down with a load you should not have to bear. Satan has reminded you of them again and again. Of course you don't understand them. But can you not commit them into God's hands? Can you not cast all your anxiety on Him since He cares so much for you (1 Peter 5:7)? You don't need to fight your own battles. You will become miserable trying to fight them, and the more you think of them, the more alone you will feel.

Forget the failures of others if you want them to forget yours. One by one you will have gathered more complaints and more proofs that your opinions about them were right. Already this has robbed you and your friends of the unity of the Spirit. Already it has hindered your prayer life. Already bitterness has begun to enter in. Your list is so long that it almost seems that you expect to be the judge on the Judgment Day!

Why bring all the past failures of others into your life now and make it impossible for God to greatly bless and use you? Why endanger God's plan for your life by holding on to all the bitter memories of the past? Bring them to the Cross just now.

Tell God all about them. Remember, you have failures too that you want others to forgive and forget.

Weep out your heart before God and truly confess to Him your own failures. Don't allow one past failure—of others or your own—to embitter your future. Bring them all to the Cross. Cover them with the precious blood of Christ. Bury them at the Cross and forget them forever.

When you forget those things, a new day will come into your life. You will really be new; your Christian experience will become new. You will have new faith and you will see new miracles as you put all of the past into the Lord's hands. You will have new strength as the Holy Spirit indwells your life in a new way. Those things that you have held on to for so long have been shutting out the fullness of His presence and His ministry. You cannot afford to go on that way any longer.

Do you want to reach forth to all those things that are ahead (Phil. 3:13)? Would you like to claim all the promises God is so longing to fulfill for you? Would you like to experience God's presence and power so that your whole life will be transformed? You can do it only as you choose to forget those things that are behind—the things the Holy Spirit has been reminding you of just now. They have been hidden in your heart too long already. Flee to the Cross and leave them there. The Holy Spirit can work so deeply in your life that you will really forget them.

The price is not too great. Your tomorrows can be the most wonderful days of your life if you will just let go of your past. Commit it all to God.

∞

Lord, teach me to forget.

Are You Singing?

Christians, sing! Sinners saved by grace, sing! Spirit-filled hearts, sing! Believers in God's promises, sing! God says, "My servants will sing out of the joy of their hearts" (Isa. 65:14). God's people are a tempted people, a tried people; often they are a suffering people—but they have always been a singing people.

Your heart can sing even when you cannot carry a tune. You can sing in your heart or repeat a song in your heart that you have memorized even when it isn't appropriate to sing aloud. Many people take a hymnbook along with their Bible during private prayer time. Try it. You will be blessed. Some verses of some gospel songs and some of the verses of the great hymns of the church are worth memorizing. Try it and use them in prayer.

He who enjoys fellowship with God soon breaks forth into singing. He who begins his day with God soon finds a song springing up within his heart. He who experiences God's guidance, God's protection, and God's help often cannot help but sound forth in some audible fashion the joy welling up within his soul.

God is the source of the Christian's singing and joy. Moses sang, "The Lord is . . . my song" (Ex. 15:2). Until you experience the new birth, until your blinded eyes are opened and your fetters of sin are shattered, you cannot know earth's greatest joy. But when your sins are forgiven, when the heavy burden of guilt and condemnation that rests upon your heart is rolled away, you can testify, "He put a new song in my mouth, a hymn of praise to our God." When this occurs, the latter part of the verse will also prove true: "Many will see and fear and put their trust in the Lord" (Ps. 40:3). Nothing is a mightier testimony to an unbelieving world than a radiant, joyous, singing Christian.

God gives us our song, and we must sing to God. At least forty-six times the Bible refers to the fact that our singing is to the Lord. We not only sing about Him, but we also sing to Him. God loves to hear the voice of His redeemed praising Him with song.

Heaven is filled with song. Angels sang before the foundation of the earth (Job 38:7). They sang at the birth of Jesus. And in eternity there will be singing in heaven (Rev. 5:9; 14:3; 15:3). Not only do the angels and the redeemed sing, but God Himself sings because of His joyful love for us (Zeph. 3:17).

The song of the Lord begins in the heart of the believer here, and it will last for all eternity. Trouble cannot stop it, darkness cannot prevent it, and suffering cannot silence it. David sang as he fled from his enemies; he sang in the long and dark night (for example, 2 Samuel 22:1). Paul and Silas sang in jail when their backs were bleeding and their feet were bound with a Roman chain (Acts 16:25). Jesus and His disciples went singing from the Upper Room to Gethsemane (Mark 14:26).

Christian, do you still have a singing heart? When you are misunderstood and misrepresented, when the circumstances seem to combine against you, when the day seems hard and long, do you indulge in self-pity and complaining? Or do you begin to sing? When you seem forgotten and forsaken, when you hesitate to mention to others the crushing burden on your heart, and when the burdens seem heavier than you can bear—do you retire to a place where you can be alone to weep? Or do you go about your tasks singing with joy in your heart to the Lord?

God has exceedingly great power. He has grace to make you more than a conqueror. He gives life and life abundant. Nothing ever takes God by surprise; He can never be defeated. He will give you not only a glass of living water, but also a river of living water within. He does not give a faith that can be used only in ordinary circumstances; He gives a mighty faith by which nothing is impossible. He puts within your heart the living power of God, the mighty Holy Spirit. He fills you with joy unspeakable and full of glory (1 Peter 1:8).

Sing for joy. Sing in spite of your problems. Singing is a way to praise the Lord. Singing and praising are ways to defeat the Devil and send him running away. Quote God's promise and sing or repeat a chorus in the face of Satan and watch him run. Do it again and again.

Lift up your head! Rejoice! Your deliverance, your answer to prayer is drawing near (Luke 21:28)! God is still on the throne! You are not forgotten by Him! Sing again this stanza of the hymn "God Moves in a Mysterious Way":

> *O fearful saints, fresh courage take;*
> *The clouds you so much dread*
> *Are big with mercy, and will break*
> *In blessings on your head.*

Lord, help me to keep singing.

"Here Am I. Send Me!"

21

Isaiah loved his nation, but now he felt crushed (Isa. 6:1–9). True, the king who had started out with the intent of making Judah great and who had greatly strengthened the nation, enlarged its borders, and defeated and silenced the enemies had given his nation new hope. King Uzziah was one of the most active, energetic, and successful kings Judah had ever had. However, he became proud, disobeyed God's command, and was eventually struck down with leprosy as punishment. Now King Uzziah had died, and the future of Judah was uncertain.

What did the future hold? Isaiah went to the temple to mourn and to pray. God suddenly gave him a glorious vision that transformed his life and ministry.

The walls of the temple seemed to fade away as he gazed up into the sky and saw God seated on His lofty throne. God's kingly, beautiful, billowing robes descended to earth and filled the temple. The heavenly seraphs worshiped God, calling, "Holy! Holy! Holy!" The temple shook as if by a mighty earthquake.

Isaiah was overwhelmed at the majesty, holiness, and glory of God. He confessed the uncleanness of his lips and those of his people. One of the seraphs flew and touched Isaiah's lips with a coal from heaven's altar, and Isaiah was forgiven and cleansed. Then suddenly he heard the voice of God. Perhaps God the Father, God the Son, and God the Holy Spirit were speaking among themselves, "Whom shall I send? And who will go for us?" Humbly, yet eagerly, Isaiah called to God, "Here am I. Send me!" And God answered him, "Go and tell" (Isa. 6:1–9). God did not call Isaiah by name: "Isaiah, will you go and give the people my message?" The voice of God had been calling out to His people, but now at last Isaiah was cleansed and had ears to hear God's voice.

God is speaking over and over in our day. Have you heard His voice? It has echoed over the centuries. It is calling to you and me today. Can you not hear Him? Are you so spiritually asleep that you have never heard Him?

I hope you attend a church in which there is real spiritual life and you have heard the reports and praise notes from time to time of how God is giving spiritual blessings in your own nation and in other parts of the world. Do you not hear God's voice through that, calling you to rejoice and praise Him for His church around the world? Do that often, asking God to bless His people in every nation.

You know something of the needs of your own country and town. You know about families who almost never go to church, homes that are breaking up, and children who are not being taught Bible stories and the truth about Jesus. Are you sufficiently spiritually awake for this to pull at your heartstrings? That is God's voice calling you to do something. Certainly you can pray for them. Make a list of the people in your own area whom you want to see brought to Jesus or who need Jesus' help. Pray for them by name each day. God's voice is calling. Do you have ears to hear? "Who will be concerned about this? Who will pray for them? Who will seek to be a blessing to them?" Listen, God's call is for you. You can answer if you choose to do so.

God also calls through events in your community—some of these events you may learn about through the conversation of neighbors and friends, some through the newspaper or radio. Do you have ears to hear God's voice in these events? Listen now!

"Whom shall I get to pray? Who will carry a prayer burden with us?" God is concerned and burdened for your community. Are you?

Additionally, God calls through the current events in the world. How loud and clear this call often is! We see warring factions in the nations, refugees fleeing for their lives and living in squalor and hunger. Jesus cares. Jesus is probably weeping today on His heavenly throne. But do you share Jesus' tears? Do you weep with Him? Or do you only say a one-sentence prayer and then forget the suffering people of the world? Do you really intercede with Jesus?

Again, God calls through the missionary reports that are filling the pages of mission magazines. Extensive missionary and evangelistic thrusts are in process right now to reach groups of people that are virtually unreached in tribes and cities where there are tremendous needs. It is exciting to see the new efforts, but, oh! what an immense volume of prayer is needed to undergird all these efforts! Haven't you heard God's voice calling you to become involved? Or have you not been getting these reports? When you support and help people in these ministries with your offerings, they will be glad to report to you.

So you and I must choose. There are wounded people and nations lying by earth's waysides. We can glance, shut our eyes, and be as involved as little as possible, like the priest and the Levite who left the wounded man on the Jericho road (Luke 10:25–37). Or we can be like the Good Samaritan and instantly respond and by our prayers and our gifts go to them and help them.

Many Christians have some knowledge of these needs but would rather not suffer the inconvenience and bother to get involved. They have never learned to care, to pray, and to love with Jesus. They disappoint Jesus. How about you? Do you really want to thrill the heart of Jesus by sharing His loving concern?

Are you close enough to God to hear His voice? Is He touching your heart now? Listen to His voice: "Whom shall I send? Who will go for us? Who will love with us? Who will join us in prayer?" You can kneel just now and say with Isaiah, "Here am I, Lord. Send me, use me, help me to love and pray!"

Or you may say, "Lord, I'm busy with my own interests. I just don't want to get involved."

Lord, help me to share Your tears and Your prayer burden. Help me to get involved.

Lord, Make Us Hungry!

How often God has given you the privilege of hearing wonderful sermons by choice servants of His! How often He has touched your heart through the words of a beautiful Christian hymn or chorus! How often you have been blessed by the fervent prayer of a Christian brother or sister! How often these things have caused sincere thanksgiving in your heart, filled you with a sense of God's presence, and given you comfort and hope! But why do the results seem so insubstantial? Why does your life seem so uniformly average? Why is it normal to be subnormal?

Undoubtedly your spiritual progress is slow, your spiritual victories so incomplete, and your spiritual blessings so quickly forgotten because you have so little spiritual hunger. We often become content with the way things are. We welcome an occasional sense of God's nearness and blessing as we would welcome a passing guest. But we don't really expect God's presence to be constantly with us. We praise God for occasional fresh anointings in His service, but we are not constantly hungering for such anointings. We are happy for the Spirit's assistance in prayer, but so often it is as easy not to pray as it is to pray. How seldom is our soul so drawn out in prayer that we hunger more for prayer and intercession than we hunger for food or sleep! How rarely do we really have thirsty souls!

So much is dependent upon spiritual hunger and thirst. God has made it a spiritual law that in order to receive one must ask. Doors do not open unless you knock, and you find only that which you really seek (Matt. 7:7). And how seldom we spiritually seek with all our heart! God's greatest spiritual blessings are indeed free, but they are nevertheless often secured only after a spiritual price is paid. This price is not related to hard effort, to vociferous praying, or to attempted earnestness. The price is not the price of effort, it is the price of hunger.

There is a sense in which God is always satisfying the spiritually hungry. There is another sense in which He longs to make us more spiritually hungry and thirsty than ever. David was a man after God's own heart because he was one whose soul literally thirsted for God, even as a deer pants for streams of water (Ps. 42:1). His soul longed for God more than watchmen long and wait for the morning (Ps. 130:6). God sets apart for Himself those who share such Godlike holy desires (Ps. 4:3).

Moses was granted a vision of God's glory because he was so insatiably hungry to see and know more of God (Ex. 33:18–19). The reason why God's glory clothed the face of Moses was that Moses was so inexpressibly hungry for more and more of God's presence, for a deeper revelation of God's very nature and being. To this day God touches with His glory those who deeply and constantly know an insatiable hunger for Him, His presence, His beauty, His holiness, and His love.

It is folly to seek God's power as one would seek an "it." It is a mistake to seek a gift from God rather than God Himself. When we have Him, we have all. The quickest way to God's power and glory is not to seek more of "it," but rather to hunger and thirst for closer and closer communion with Him. It is He the Holy Spirit whom we need in all His perfect indwelling.

Oh, let us know more of Him! Let us not hunger for "success," for "power," or for any other kind of "it." Let us hunger for more of Him, because if we hunger for Him with an insatiable hunger, God will flood our lives with Himself and we will have more than we have ever asked or thought. No eye has seen, no ear has heard all that God longs to be to us, but He reveals this to us by His Spirit (1 Cor. 2:9–10).

Lord, make us really hungry, insatiably hungry, for You!

Do You Embarrass God?

Have you ever wondered if your life has not been more of an embarrassment to God than a contribution to His cause? There is too great a tendency to put a halo over the heads of those who are recognized by the public as having set themselves apart for the work of God. Are some of God's ambassadors an embarrassment to the kingdom they claim to represent?

Have you ever surveyed your life in some quiet moment of meditation to see whether you really deserve a place in God's roll of heroes? Some of your friends continue to put you on that roster regardless of how much you may personally disclaim anything worthy of special mention. There are young lives being patterned after you. There are many observing you who place you in a special category whether you want it or not.

Do you claim to be a Christian? Then the people of the world demand a higher standard of life from you than they expect from themselves. Are you called a Christian leader? Then what great expectations God, the church, and the world have for your life!

Does your life really show that you are a child of God? Christ's claim to be the Son of God glorified God because He was God manifest in the flesh. Do you claim to be a child of God? Then godliness should be the outstanding mark of your life. Does your life serve as an obvious illustration of what the God of Christians is like? If you are born of God, you must have and exhibit something of the nature of God—not in its manifestation of supernatural power but in its manifestation of Godlike love, patience, holiness, mercy, kindness, and truth. Does the lack of practical godliness in your daily life and work ever embarrass God your Father?

So you are a Christian—one like Christ, a veritable "little Christ" (say it reverently)? Then your life should light the world just as He is the Light of the World. You should be silent in the face of accusation as He was silent. You should be as ready to empty yourself of all in which you might glory even as He gladly emptied Himself of His eternal glory. You should as steadfastly set your face to bear a cross as He set His face to bear Calvary's cross.

Your life should be one of saving others rather than yourself. Your prayer should daily be "not my will but Yours be done." You should manifest the love that never weakens, never tires, never avoids, and never fails regardless of the suffering involved. Does your being a Christian beautify, magnify, and interpret the name of Christ to the world; or is it an embarrassment to Christ?

Fellow Christian! How long have you and I claimed to follow Christ? Then why are we still following Him at such an embarrassing distance? Why are we so embarrassingly un-Christlike in our thought life, in our conversation, and in our hours of pressure and temptation?

May God deliver us from the shame of Christian mediocrity, of subapostolic character, subapostolic love, and subapostolic witness. May He make us ambassadors who will commend Him by our lives rather than embarrass the King and the kingdom of the God we claim to represent.

Prayer: O God, so long we have sought and prayed for extensive revival. Please begin that revival by making Your supernatural work intensely personal in each one of us. Begin Your miracle before the world by Your miracle in me.

∞

Lord, may I not embarrass You today!

We Need a Revival of Love

Thank God, there is a way by which your Christian friends can be sure that your testimony is genuine. There is a way by which those who have heard false reports about you will know that they should not believe them. There is a way by which worldly people and non-Christian friends will be sure that Christ has performed a miracle in your life. It is the way of love.

Love can always manifest itself in your service and in your conduct with those you seek to influence. Love can always be manifest in the tone of your voice, in the look on your face, in the manner with which you meet with children and adults, your friends, and your enemies. Your love will always show.

As a Christian you should be more faithful to duty than others are. If you do not do more than your duty, you dishonor the name of Christ. But as a Christian you serve for a far deeper reason than to be a good witness. You serve because you love. You serve through your love. All you say and do is made different by your love. Your Christlikeness is proved above all else by your love.

The Bible commands us to "serve one another in love" (Gal. 5:13). In our Christian relations with our fellow believers our outstanding characteristic should be love. This love should not be merely love in name, but a love that serves (1 John 3:18). It is thus a humble love, a love that is willing to not have its own way, a love that is willing to take a lowly place while someone else is exalted. We have Christian liberty, Paul reminds us. We should not be in bondage to anyone else. But this Christian liberty should be proved by the way we serve others with Christlike love.

This contrast is made even more clear in Galatians 5:15: "If you keep on biting and devouring each other, watch out or you will be destroyed by each other." There are those who try to prove that they have liberty and are not in bondage to others; they do so by being independent of others, by saying what is on their minds, by making cutting remarks. This does not prove liberty; rather, it proves bondage.

A person who has liberty is able to ignore the slights, the taunts, and even the injustice of others. He who is in bondage cannot fully love; he tends to bite and devour. He who lives in liberty has the power to love in spite of what others do against him. He is able to forgive and forget. He is able to suffer long and still be kind. He is too big of soul to resent or hold a grudge. It is the little, tiny, shriveled-up souls who have to react carnally to the evil words and actions of others.

A dog that is tied up often develops a bad disposition. He wants to growl, snarl, and bite. Whatever a dog's disposition is, it usually gets worse when he is tied up. A soul that is in bondage reacts the same way. The Christian who answers a disagreeable word with a disagreeable word is like a tied-up, snarling dog. He proves that he is in bondage to his carnal self. He proves that he does not love as he ought to love.

As a Christian, if you really love, you will answer an insult with words of blessing (see 1 Peter 2:9). You will answer a hateful glance with a smile. You will answer cursing with prayer (Rom. 12:14). You will answer injustice by serving the unjust one with Christian love (see 1 Cor. 4:12). No one but a Christian can do this, and that is why such love is always a powerful Christian testimony. This is not mere theory. It works! Nothing is so powerful as that kind of love.

Do you want to prove the reality of your Christian love? Prove it by your reactions in the most trying circumstances. Prove it by your overcoming evil with good, by your overcoming hate with love. Prove that there is no injustice so great but that the love of God in you is greater. Prove that there is no enemy who can compel you to hate him—you will not be brought into bondage to anyone, you will love them in spite of all they do against you. Prove Christ true by proving that your love is greater than all else.

The biggest proof of your Christian love, however, is not in the major crises of your life. The greatest and most convincing proof of your love is often in the little details of your daily life. The biggest testimony of your life is not the way you react to unfriendly people of the world, or to non-Christians who do not understand you and who oppose you. Rather, the biggest proof of the reality of your Christian love is the way you prove it to your fellow-Christians, to your family, to your co-workers, to those who work most intimately with you.

You may profess to love those outside the church, but they will not believe you until you prove your love for the people you know well. Christians may profess their love for the whole world, but until they have full unity in their local church, who will believe them? The quarrels among brethren in the local church bring only pain to Jesus and disgrace to His name.

The average unsaved person is hindered by quarrels among Christians more than by the existence of many churches. Loving unity within your local church is always the will of God. Denominations need to appoint committees to go from church to church to bring unity among ministers, unity among ministers and congregations, and unity among quarreling groups within local congregations.

The existence of one misunderstanding or quarrel between two Christian brothers or sisters should be enough for every deacon, elder, or member of the local church committee to humble himself before God and to fast, weep, and pray until unity is restored. The existence of one quarrel in a church is enough to keep the pastor on his face in burdened intercession, weeping and pleading before God for his people until love is once again restored. Pastors should be so broken-hearted over any breach of love in their churches that a restoration

of love becomes a major priority. District superintendents, modera-
tors, and bishops should be so tenderhearted that in any church where
they find such divisions they should weep with the pastor before God
and perhaps the congregation. Jesus Christ wept over Jerusalem. He
who is not brokenhearted over quarrels among Christians does not
have the heart of a pastor or a shepherd and certainly does not have
the heart of Christ.

Organization is important, but love is all-important. The prime
responsibility of church leaders is not just to keep the organization
running smoothly, not just to preside over committees—it is to
restore love to Christian groups, Christian homes, and Christian
hearts. Let us not deceive ourselves. Nothing is more important than
love. Nothing more dishonors the cause of Christ than lack of love.
Nothing does more to keep the unsaved away from Christ and
doubting our testimonies than lack of love. Nothing robs us of the
power of the Holy Spirit more than tension and disunity.

We need to see a revival of love sweep through our churches, through our organizations, and through our homes. Love is our
greatest need. Love must come first in our lives. We must serve one
another in love. We must love those outside the church too, by all
means. But what good is it to profess to love them when we do
not have love among ourselves?

Let us humble ourselves before God. Let us acknowledge our
need. Let us put first things first. Let us humble ourselves before one
another. Let us ask forgiveness. Let us take the blame upon ourselves.
Let us become so humble that we will do much more than merely
tolerate one another but by love actually serve one another. By this
Christ will be exalted, by this our church life will be revived, and by
this a new and powerful testimony will go forth before the unsaved.

"A new command I give you: Love one another. As I have
loved you, so you must love one another. By this all men will know
that you are my disciples, if you love one another" (John 13:34–35).

∞

Lord, give us fullness of holy love.

Every Christian a Priest

The only way in which the church of Jesus Christ will be able to fulfill God's call for it is to realize in a new way its responsibility as a holy, royal priesthood to God. To be Christian in the truly scriptural sense is to be a priest of God. No person has a right to call himself or herself a Christian without conscientiously seeking day by day to be a faithful priest of God.

There is no New Testament basis for ordaining one Christian as a priest on behalf of other Christians. It is scriptural to ordain elders and to have deacons and bishops in the church, but there is no scriptural office of a priest in the New Testament. Every Christian is a priest of God.

In spite of the strong emphasis of the Reformation on each Christian as a believer-priest, Protestantism has not yet rid itself of the unscriptural attitude that some are ordained and paid to do the witnessing and praying for others. A paid ministry that exercises spiritual oversight is in accordance with the teaching of the New Testament, but there is no provision for a paid priesthood.

We who are leaders of the people of God need to repent and ask God's forgiveness for our failure to develop every true Christian into an active witness and an interceding priest. No person has the right to call himself a New Testament Christian unless he is both a witness and a priest.

No church has the right to stop instructing a convert until he is a victorious witness and a prevailing intercessor. It is just as essential for a new Christian to be taught to intercede as it is for him to be taught basic doctrine. We have been commanded far more often to pray than to assemble for group worship. Both, however, are scriptural.

It was God's plan for Israel to be a kingdom of priests (Ex. 19:6). Every true Israelite was to have been holy in life and set apart for God to mediate His blessings and to shed His light to the ends of the earth. Israel failed to be God's witnesses to the world and failed to be God's intercessors. The experience of Job should have taught Israel that God would deliver them when they prayed for their surrounding neighboring nations, even as God restored Job's fortune when he prayed for his friends.

In the very same prophecy of Isaiah in which Christ's earthly ministry was set forth (Isa. 61:1–3) it was prophesied that Zion's children would be called the "priests of the Lord . . . ministers of our God" (v. 6). It was made very clear that the prophesied days when all God's people would be priests were the days of the church, for Isaiah said that even the Gentiles would take the place of the Old Testament priests and Levites (66:21). It is on this basis that Peter said we are "a chosen people, a royal priesthood, a holy nation" (1 Peter 2:9), and "a holy priesthood, offering spiritual sacrifices acceptable to God through Jesus Christ" (v. 5).

Christ is our High Priest "after the order of Melchizedek." This is of such importance that it is mentioned six times in Scripture. The New Testament Christian is a believer-priest in the order of Melchizedek even as Christ is the High Priest in that order. This is proved by three things: (1) Melchizedek, Christ, and we believers are not of the Aaronic line of priests but are called and appointed by God for this ministry. (2) Melchizedek, Christ, and we are royal priests. Peter declared, "But you are . . . a royal priesthood" (1 Peter 2:9). Christ has made us a kingdom and priests unto God

(Rev. 1:6). (3) Melchizedek, Christ, and we have an unending priest-hood (Heb. 7:1–3, 24–25; Rev. 5:10).

As priests to God we offer spiritual sacrifices of praise and thanksgiving (Heb. 13:15) and the fourfold aspect of priestly inter-cession outlined in 1 Timothy 2:1—requests, prayers, intercession, and thanksgiving. We are told that we are "first of all" responsible for making priestly intercession for everyone. But this is one aspect of Christian responsibility in which the church is so spiritually immature and unspiritual that the full revelation of the responsi-bility of our priesthood is understood and taught by few (Heb. 5:11–14).

Many Christians rejoice over the fact that Christ has, by His death on the cross, opened a new and living way into the very pres-ence of God and that every Christian now has immediate access to God's presence (Heb. 10:19–22). But few realize that this is not primarily a means to get personal favors from God, but that it is pri-marily a priestly access to God in which the high-priestly rights have been given to us and that with Christ we are therefore to live to intercede for others.

Few people realize that the torn curtain of the temple puts them under solemn obligation to God to be priestly intercessors for the whole world and particularly for the church of God, even as Christ makes this His main and eternal ministry. Our access to God is primarily for the sake of others. It is indeed a wonderful privi-lege for which we should all rejoice; however, it is also a privilege that confers on us one of our most solemn obligations to God.

The Christian is in the world to be a priest who intercedes for the world. Any Christian who prays only for himself is not truly a New Testament Christian. He is certainly not Christlike, for Christ maintained a continuing prayer ministry for others during His earthly life and He does this above all else today. There is no more Christlike ministry than the ministry of intercession. No Christ-ian has fulfilled his scriptural responsibility on any given day if he has not been an intercessory priest for others that day.

No Christian can fulfill his missionary obligation as given him by Christ (Matt. 28:19–20; Acts 1:8) unless he daily intercedes for the whole world. He may go as a witness to some, he may reach yet others by his tithes and offerings, but only through prayer can he personally reach the whole world.

Many Christians live as though they will not be responsible for the rest of the world at the judgment seat of God. But if Scripture teaches anything, it teaches us our responsibility for the world. Many Christians, even many missionaries, are living failures in the sight of God because they have never realized their responsibility as priests to intercede for all mankind. No Christian is a biblical Christian, no Christian is a biblical priest if his or her prayers, intercessions, and thanksgivings do not frequently include people in all countries.

Christ commanded every Christian to pray—not only for himself, but also for others. Paul and the early leaders of the Christian church expected every Christian to pray. The Bible says far more about the universal duty of praying than about the duty of giving. Yet many church leaders feel duty bound to teach all their people to give but seldom recognize their duty to teach every Christian to live a life of intercession for others.

There is no Christian duty that so leads to growth in grace as that of intercession for others. It develops in the soul those Christlike graces of love, sympathy, gentleness, long-suffering, tenderness, and mercy. There is no Christian activity that is so productive of unity, love, and Christlikeness among God's people as this priestly ministry of intercession.

No Christian is a biblical Christian unless he carries the burdens of others. This is the great law of Christ (Gal. 6:2). No one can do more in bearing the burdens of others than by praying. No one can bear the burdens of more people in any other way. We must do more than pray, of course, but no activity so motivates other Christian activity as does prayer. No Christian activity unites one with Christ as does intercession. No Christian activity is more Christlike than that of prayer for others.

Failure in intercession is perhaps the most basic and tragic failure of the church. We must find a new way to enlist every Christian into a full New Testament priesthood. Only in this way will the church become ablaze with evangelistic passion and zeal. Only in this way will the Gospel reach every person. Only in this way will the Christian be kept victorious in his own life and constantly prove to be God's salt and light in the earth. Only in this way will the Christian become fully one with Christ in heart, ministry, and love.

Every pastor, every church leader, every Bible teacher, every evangelist, every Christian leader of any kind must give new priority to leading the people of God into a Christlike priesthood of intercession. Every church and missionary society must realize its solemn obligation before God to labor night and day until Christian priestly intercession becomes the normal life of every member of the church of Christ.

God will hold you responsible for your own ministry of intercession and for leading others into the fulfillment of this biblical command. This is one of the reasons why you are alive today by the mercy of God. This is one of the reasons why God has placed you where you serve Him today. The church must be set ablaze once more, and the world must be reached with the touch of Christ. Christian, LET US PRAY!

∞

Lord, make me Your faithful priest for the world.

What Nation
Are You Asking For?

26

"Ask of me, and I will make the nations your inheritance, the ends of the earth your possession" (Ps. 2:8). This is the command and promise of God the Father to Jesus, His Messiah Son. Jesus was to inherit the nations—not by conquest by the sword, but by intercession, by Jesus' asking.

This is what Jesus our High Priest is fulfilling today. This is His role, His divine assignment until He comes again. He is seated at the right hand of God on heaven's throne (Heb. 8:1). He has been exalted to the position of sovereign of the universe. He is to reign by intercession until He comes for us. He is to conquer and to win the nations by asking for them.

So Jesus ever lives to intercede (Heb. 7:25). Intercession is prayer for others, blessing others by prayer that makes requests for them. Today Jesus is asking for the nations—asking for them nation by nation. What a revelation it would be if we could hear the actual words of Jesus as He asks for and pleads for each individual people.

God did not plan for Jesus to intercede alone. God planned that Jesus would be the High Priest over a whole priesthood. God chose that every child of His would be not only a member of the family of God but also a member of His royal priesthood. "You are a chosen people, a royal priesthood" (1 Peter 2:9). Jesus' blood has freed us from our sins and made us to be priests to God (Rev. 1:5–6).

The high priest needs assisting priests. You and I are to assist Jesus by our priestly intercession. The Old Testament high-priestly responsibility was to mediate by offering sacrifices and by intercession. At the cross Jesus offered Himself as the perfect sacrifice that fulfilled all redemptive sacrifices. "It is finished," Jesus cried. Christ's sacrifice was His finished work. Intercession is the unfinished work of Christ—the work to which He devotes Himself unceasingly today and to which He summons you and me. Intercession is His primary work now and, as His royal helping priests, we are to join Him in that intercession. In our joint intercession He becomes the Amen of God (Rev. 3:14). We intercede with Him and through Him, and He seals our prayers with His "amen."

In this dispensation Jesus asks for the people of the nations and for national groupings. Jesus won the battle of the ages in Gethsemane and on the cross. The redemptive price is complete. Now the battle is to apply that redemptive victory in place after place and in individual lives, as each person is led to make his or her own appropriation of Calvary's victory. Christ intercedes, and so should we. As we join in holy intercession in Jesus' name for person after person, we are His royal priests.

Ask for persons, ask for families, ask for towns and cities, ask for nations. Do you know what it is to wrestle in prayer for a person or for a nation? Have you an extensive daily prayer list? Are you carrying a daily intercessory burden for one or more nations and peoples?

Ask the Holy Spirit to guide you. There is holy joy in being faithful to the prayer needs God the Spirit has placed on your heart and has assigned to you. The more faithful you are in your intercession, the deeper will be the hunger that the Holy Spirit shares with you. Have you often seen people weep in their intercession as they fulfilled Psalm 2:8? I have no more precious memory of my mother than that of seeing her on her knees interceding with sobs and tears day after day as she loved, hungered for, and asked for China and India. I am sure thousands of Chinese and Indian people will come to her and thank her in heaven for her love, prayers, and tears.

On the day you stand before Christ's glorious throne to receive your eternal reward, may God reward you abundantly for your holy intercessions. May you be introduced to persons and national groups as one of those who faithfully and lovingly hungered and interceded for them and their land day after day. God grant that with shining faces they may come to you, thank you, embrace you, and welcome you as one of God's great gifts to them.

Oh, you will be eternally glad for every person on your prayer list, for every prayer burden you carried, and every loving tear you shed. Don't miss the special joys of that glorious Judgment Day when you will be rewarded for all your intercessory prayer. Don't forget to ask for nations from today on.

Lord, teach me to intercede with Christ.

Measure Your Mountain by God

Mountains spell challenge; mountains spell opportunity; mountains spell miracle when God is with you.

Mountains were created to get people to look up, not down. Mountains are meant to challenge us, not to discourage us. God could have created a level world, a world where everything would be easy—but He created a world with mountains.

Perhaps you are facing a mountain of difficulty now. Perhaps the situation you face seems more hopeless and impossible than any you have previously faced. Every place in the world is a harvest field for God. Perhaps God has permitted you to labor in a hard harvest field where results seem impossible. Servant of God, look up, believe God, pray once more; God can move your mountain!

We live in a day when there is less ground for discouragement than ever before. We live in a day when people can do in their own strength the things long thought impossible. The world's highest mountain has been scaled. Man has walked on the moon. We send our voice around the world in a moment of time. In spiritual things we have the record of more answers to prayer to encourage our faith than any previous generation ever had. Means of communication have so improved that Christians of one country know more about those of other countries than ever before.

How do you know but that some humble child of God is just now on his knees praying for you? How do you know but that some child of God who speaks some other language is now wrestling with God in prayer, bearing an unknown burden, believing for an unknown victory that God has placed on his heart for you? He may never hear your name till he gets to heaven. You may never get to thank him until you meet at Jesus' feet.

God knows how to network prayer. Take courage; thank God. You are not alone in the battle! Do not stare in despair at the mountain before you. Look up to its lofty height; look up above it to your mighty God. Challenge your mountain in prayer. "Say to this mountain, 'Move from here to there' and it will move. Nothing will be impossible for you" (Matt. 17: 20–21).

Mountains are God-given opportunities! Mountains give you a chance to watch God work! Mountains give God a chance to enlist a mighty volume of prayer from many other prayer warriors on your behalf. Perhaps all you see are the iron chariots of the enemy covering the mountainside. Do you feel like crying with Elisha's servant, "What shall we do?" Be encouraged. Elisha told his servant, "Don't be afraid. . . . Those who are with us are more than those who are with them" (2 Kings 6:15–16). Let God open your eyes, and you will see an even mightier host of chariots of fire to help and protect you.

Do you feel as if the soil on which you have been sowing is barren, hard, and unwatered? Be encouraged! Just beyond yonder mountain lie fertile valleys, flowing streams, abundant harvests. Mountains are like doors; mountains are God's opportunities. Conquer your mountain, and the abundance beyond will be yours.

Don't measure the harvest to come by the harvest you have known. Pray to the Lord of the harvest once more. Believe with a mighty faith. Challenge your mountain with conquering prayer. Perhaps all that keeps you from a harvest is your need to learn how to move that mountain by believing prayer.

Mountains mean miracle when God is with you. Don't measure your mountain by the weakness of your past life. God wants to make you mightier than you have ever been before. Don't measure your mountain by your present circumstances. God wants to do something new to the praise of His glory. Measure your mountain by the omnipotence of God. Measure your mountain by the faithfulness of His Word. Measure your mountain by the glory it will bring to God when He has moved it.

The greater the impossibility, the greater the possibility of glory to God. Why be satisfied with the ordinary when you have the right to God's miracle power? Why rest content with drudgery when you can have God's glory? Abandon yourself to God as never before. Dare to challenge your mountain! You can have a miracle if you dare to claim it from God. God is not man; God is not weak; God is almighty. Your situation is never too hard for God. Mountains—your mountains—can become glorious miracles, for God is with you!

Lord, help me to measure my mountains by You!

Let the Word Dwell in You

Does the Word of Christ literally live in you? Do you literally live in the Word? Just as truly as Christ lives in His own people and they live in Him, so His Word can live in them and they can live in His Word. Oh, the unspeakable blessing of a life in which these words of Paul are fulfilled: "Let the word of Christ dwell in you richly" (Col. 3:16).

The Word can never dwell in you unless you take time for reading the Scriptures. How can a person claim to love Christ when he spends almost no time reading His Word? One may spend hours in talking to friends and listening to what others have to say. How dare Christians claim to love Christ greatly if they spend less than fifteen minutes a day with the Bible and listening to the voice of God?

No believer should read the New Testament through less than once a year! If one reads the Bible an average of three chapters per weekday and five per Sunday, he will finish the entire Bible in less than a year. What minister or Christian worker can consider himself faithful who does less? We cannot have the Word dwelling in us if we do not take the time to read the Bible through systematically. What an insult to God for one to have been a Christian for years and still not have read His Word systematically!

There is no reading thrill to compare with the thrill one gets from reading the Bible through repeatedly, especially the New Testament. Each time you complete a reading of the Bible you will find your heart leaping for joy. There is spiritual strength you obtain from God's Word that can be obtained in no other way. There is no faith tonic so miraculous as feeding on the Scriptures. "Faith comes from hearing the message, and the message is heard through the word of Christ" (Rom. 10:17).

No Christian in good spiritual health will ever tire of the Word. When you have read the Bible through twenty-five times, you will wish it had been fifty. What a joy to complete the fiftieth, one hundredth, or two hundredth reading of the New Testament! Often, as you complete a reading, you will wonder if you have not received more blessing in this reading of the Word than you have ever received in a previous reading of it.

Some parts of the Old Testament, especially where there are long lists of names, do not especially bless you as you read them. Some passages, such as those that give instructions for the Old Testament sacrifices or the dimensions of the temple, may yield comparatively little blessing, but they do help you realize how detailed God's guidance can be, even in our lives today. Most historical passages and prophetic passages do have much to teach us.

What you have read repeatedly can easily be brought to your memory again by the Holy Spirit, and He may use this to guide you, correct you, or build your confidence and faith.

There is something exceedingly precious in the Word of God. No delicious meal is so satisfying as receiving a blessing from God's Word. No music is so wonderful as that which springs up within your soul from verses of Scripture that seem to be a direct message from God to you. No adventure is so thrilling as finding a new revelation of Christ and His will in the Word. No wealth is so lasting as the riches of Christ and His Word.

Oh, friend, feast on God's Word, drink from the fountains of blessing in the Scriptures. Taste and see the blessings in store for you. Lean upon God's promises. Light your pathway with light from the sacred pages.

If you would have peace, read the Word. If you would have faith, read the Word. If you would chase away the Devil, take the sword of the Spirit, which is the Word of God (Eph. 6:17). If you would have joy, read the Word. If you want your prayer life transformed, read God's Word. If you want all the riches of Christ, let His Word dwell in you richly, and you too will break forth into song, with music and hymns and blessings flooding and filling your soul (5:19).

∽

Lord, help me live deeply in Your Word.

I Am with You

This is Christ's wonderful message for you today: "Surely I am with you always" (Matt. 28:20). It is a lesson as important for you now as it was for the disciples in the first century. After the Crucifixion they had become overwhelmed with a sense of loss. They mourned an absent Christ. The Christ who had come to them, the Christ who had lived with them, the Christ they loved was gone. He seemed gone from their lives, gone from their ministry, gone from their future. They were alone; Christ was gone.

Then, suddenly, the Resurrection brought an incredible message. Christ was not gone—He was more truly with them than ever before. Mary wept at the tomb, but suddenly she found Christ was with her in her sorrow, and her sorrow was turned to comfort and joy. Cleopas and another disciple longed for Him as they walked along the road, and suddenly they found that Christ was with them in their home and had been with them on their journey.

The disciples hid in an upper room. They were frightened and confused. Suddenly they found that Christ was in their midst to banish their fear and confusion. Thomas, who had not been with them then, said he would not believe until he saw—and a week later Christ was there to prove that He was God. Some of the disciples needed guidance; they tried a night of fishing, but this ended in failure and discouragement. Suddenly Christ was with them beside the lake with guidance, success, refreshment, and a commission.

This was absolutely transforming for the disciples. At any moment Christ might manifest Himself visibly to them—along the road, in their own home, in their services, in their work. They had been thinking of Christ exclusively as a localized Christ; He had told them that wherever two or three were gathered together in His name He was present with them, but they had not yet understood this. Now they were suddenly made aware of the fact that He might manifest Himself to them at any time and in any place.

Yet they had one more step to take. They needed one more step to understand that whether they saw Him or not He was with them all the time and in every place. And so to make sure that they fully understood and would never forget this, Christ's final words of the Great Commission were the words of this great assurance, "Surely I am with you always."

Do you live today as though the Resurrection has not occurred? Do you today think, live, serve, and even pray as though Christ were an absent Christ? The great reality of the Resurrection is that Christ, though invisible, is always present. You may not be conscious of His presence. He may not manifest Himself to you because of your spiritual dullness, but He is always with you. He is always present; He is always available to you. You are never alone.

Christ is always with you as a loving Person. He is ever by your side; He is ever ready to fellowship with you. He always sees you, He always hears you, He always cares for you. You are never in a situation where He is not with you. He is always loving you, always sharing in your life. He is always waiting to hear your voice, always ready to let you feel His presence. In the loneliest hour, in the most difficult trial, in the greatest responsibility, in your most intimate joys, in your deepest disappointments—always, always He is with you.

Christ is always with you in all His resurrection power. He is with you, triumphing over Satan, sin, temptation, and death itself. He is always with you as the mighty God, the miracle-working Savior, the One to whom all things are easy. He needs but to speak, and worlds leap into existence, nature obeys, demons flee, and all the resources of heaven are brought into action. He needs but to speak, and instantly thousands of angels hasten to obey and to serve you for His sake.

You may be totally insufficient, but the Sufficient One is with you. All authority in heaven and earth is His. He is with you as your most beloved One, but He is also with you as Lord of heaven and earth.

The resurrection message is that the almighty Lord is with you. You do not need to be strong in yourself, for He is with you. You do not need to be wise in yourself, for He is with you. Don't worry about resources at your disposal, for He is with you. How glorious, how faith-inspiring, how wonderful!

Walk into your future humbled, but with your head held high. The sovereign Lord of heaven and earth is with you. The Lord is your light and your salvation—whom should you fear? The Lord is the strength of your life—why should you be afraid (Ps. 27:1)? Though you face the lion's den, He is with you; though you must contest the entire host of Satan, He is with you. One word from Him, and demons must flee in confusion! One word from Him, and the very powers of nature must obey!

Courage, fellow Christian! Walk into your future singing the praises of God! Let Easter's message be your daily song—He lives, He is with you. Let Easter joy be your daily strength. Jesus has not gone away—Jesus is as truly with you today as He is with the Father. You are walking with Him as truly as Cleopas did on the Emmaus road. When you kneel to pray, Jesus joins in your intercession. When the tears flow down your cheek, they flow down His also. When you have toiled all night and have taken nothing, He is as ready to tell you where to cast the net as He was when He aided Peter and the other disciples.

Let the Christ of Easter speak to your heart today, "SURELY I AM WITH YOU ALWAYS!" Rejoice with Easter joy; believe with a triumphant Easter faith; go forth with the glorious Easter witness: HE LIVES! HE LIVES! Go forth in the power of His resurrection and the glory of His presence and your heart, too, will burn within you as He walks with you in the way He has chosen for you. Oh, believe it, live it, proclaim it! This is His personal word to you: "Surely I am with you" (Matt. 28:20).

Lord, help me sense Your living presence today.

 Arise, Shine!

It is time for all of us to begin to live evangelistically. Evangelism is something we must do with both our lives and our lips. Neither form of evangelism is complete without the other. No Christian is excused from either type of evangelistic responsibility. Whether man or woman, old or young, layman or clergyman—everyone must have a witnessing life and witnessing lips.

The New Testament presents a pattern of clear-cut, comprehensive, and constant evangelism. Neither Christ nor the early church camouflaged their purpose. Evangelism must extend to every person in every nation. A salvation that delivers from every sin must be proclaimed.

Every thought and motive must be brought into obedience to Christ (2 Cor. 10:5). Spirit, soul, and body must be presented in a total consecration (1 Thess. 5:23). The church must be cleansed until it is without stain, wrinkle, or any other blemish (Eph. 5:27). There is no stopping place until we all attain the whole measure of the fullness of God (3:19). When Jesus returns, every believer will be presented perfect in Christ (Col. 1:28).

In order to attain this purpose the life of every Christian must be definitely and ultimately evangelistic. Your eyes and mine must radiate an evangelist's love. Our lips must speak the Savior's praise and voice the Savior's invitation. Our hands must bless with a redemptive touch. Our feet must bring good tidings wherever we go. Our hearts must throb with a passion for the lordship of Christ and the salvation of people. The vision of Christ must become our vision; His passion for God's kingdom must become our passion. His will must have preeminence; His kingdom must be priority number one in our lives.

This does not mean that every act can or should be directly and immediately evangelistic. We must live useful, practical lives. We must rejoice with those who rejoice and weep with those who weep (Rom. 12:15). We must teach, heal, and serve others. Jesus needs us, and people also need us.

We should not make every conversation a sermon, or every act an attempt to convert. But the underlying motive and passion twenty-four hours a day in you and me should be that others may see and understand Christ. The constant prayer-breath of our soul should be that people seeing our good works may see not us but Christ. My all-pervading desire, your all-consuming passion, should be that all may know our wonderful Savior, too.

When all of life is saturated with redemptive love, with the evangelist's passion, witnessing with our words will be as natural as breathing. The witness may be only a "God bless you"; it may be only a "I feel so happy today; Christ was so near in prayer this morning"; or "I am so sorry; I will remember this (or you) in prayer." But you will never hesitate to explain the reason for your joy, your faith, and your inner strength.

There is an insidious danger in the "influence theory" of evangelism; that is in letting the life speak for itself without witnessing with the lips. But when life and lips witness together, all of life can be a seeking of God's kingdom first.

"Arise, shine. . . . See, darkness covers the earth and thick darkness is over the peoples, but the Lord rises upon you and his glory appears over you" (Isa. 60:1–2).

If you rise and shine, then those about you "will come to your light."

∞

Lord, use me as an evangelist today.

Will Revival
Come Through You?

Revival always comes from God, but it also always comes through a person of God. God has chosen to make His kingdom and His glory to a certain extent dependent on you. If you do not experience continuous personal revival in your own heart, God will fail to receive His full glory, His kingdom will suffer, and you will lose the reward God desires to bestow on you.

Every great movement of God in real revival has been marked by His use of the prevailing prayer of many prayer warriors as they obeyed God's call to prayer. It has also involved His anointing of a few chosen leaders.

Often the rivers of revival blessings that transform the barren deserts into gardens of God are fed by numerous hidden streams. The foundations for every great work of God go much deeper than is apparent to the human eye.

Before God demonstrates His mighty power publicly, He calls His saints to pray and humble themselves alone before Him. Before God manifests His transcendent glory in His church, He gives His hidden ones hungry hearts. Every hunger and thirsting in your heart for God's revival power and glory is proof of God's desire to bless and work exceedingly above your small comprehension. Every such passionate desire in your soul should make you pray, believe, and praise as never before. This is clear evidence that God desires to use you as one of His instruments for revival.

Our greatest need is not for revival leadership. God always raises up His chosen instrument when the hour is fully come. God often chooses His leaders from the most unlikely of places. Any one of a multitude of people could be God's chosen leader in revival if he or she is utterly and fully yielded to God.

No one can be God's leader in revival unless he or she is God-anointed. That means that the glory and miracle power are God's alone. Every past or present leader in genuine revival will gladly and repeatedly admit that he was neither able nor worthy of the position into which God thrust him. God uses such people so that the glory may be totally His own. No, our greatest need is not for some great leader.

Our greatest need is for people like you and me to faithfully carry a burden of prayer. Our greatest need is for adequate hidden sources for revival. Revival will come only when there are enough hungry hearts, enough pleading intercessors, enough saints who will weep as they pray, enough who will be desperate enough to fast and pray. God has chosen to make His children a kingdom and priests (Rev. 1:6). They are to be ready always to intercede—in a constant fellowship with their Lord because He always lives to intercede (Heb. 7:25).

God could have chosen otherwise, but He has chosen that the prayer of a righteous person will be powerful and effective. He has chosen that we will not have until we ask, that we will not have an open door until we knock, that we will not find until we seek. God always does far beyond what we ask for, but He nevertheless says, "You do not have, because you do not ask God" (James 4:2).

We are living in the Holy Spirit's dispensation, in the church age, in the revival age. We have not yet even begun to realize all that God longs to do for and through His church. You are a part of that church. You have not even begun to realize all that God can do for and through you. You will either help or hinder revival, you will either be an instrument of the Holy Spirit to help bring about revival or you will bring grief to the Holy Spirit. Which will it be? To what extent are you willing to pay the spiritual price that revival may come at least partly through you?

Lord, use my intercession to prepare Your way for revival.

Money Is so Sacred

Money can be filthy and defiling. Money can also be a sacred love-gift. Giving money with holy hands and a loving heart can be spiritual worship of God. Money can express the deepest longing of your heart and the sweet adoration of your spirit as you give it to Jesus. You can use your money to show your love to God.

In the sight of God it is not the size of your gift but the love with which it is given that makes it so precious to Him. Nothing touches the heart of God more than the widow's mite. But who gives the widow's mite today? The widow Jesus praised for her love-gift gave all that she had to live on.

It was the same quality of love that caused Mary to take a year's wages, purchase the most costly perfume, and then break the alabaster box and pour it all on Jesus' head and feet (John 12:3). A gift like that cannot be measured in dollars and cents. It can be measured partly in the tears that rained down on Jesus' feet. But only God could measure it in the depths of her loving heart.

Have you ever given to God a gift so costly that others criticized you for giving too much, but you gave it because you loved God so much you could not bear to give less? Have you given it with tears of love—tears of love for Him who died for you? with tears of joy because you gave something so precious in His sight? Oh, what holy joy there is in giving because we love Jesus so much!

Giving money not only expresses love, but can also be a sacred prayer. The amount does not necessarily measure its prayer fragrance in the presence of God. You may give a hundred dollars and it may tell God more of your lack of vision, lack of concern, and lack of sacrifice than of the depth of these qualities. It may be that in His sight real vision, real concern, real sacrifice on your part could not have led you to give less than a thousand dollars.

On the other hand, it may be that your gift of ten dollars reveals to God real vision, deep concern, and costly sacrifice. Your ten dollars may have prayer-fragrance before God that tells how deeply you long to do more. It is your heart that counts!

You cannot love without giving something. If you love God and if you love people in need, you will long to give. You will rejoice with every additional gift. Giving means loving. You cannot give less than prayer. You certainly are not loving if you do not pray!

You cannot love without longing to give financially to God's cause—for the sake of the salvation of people and for the glory of Jesus' name. If you do not long to give more than you can give, your love is inadequate. God measures your gift by your longing.

If all we are and all we have are consecrated to God, if we love Him with all our heart, all our soul, and all our strength, then our heart will long to meet every new need, and our lives will be filled with joy when we can give. Why did Jesus sit and watch the people give their offerings for God's cause? Because giving is sacred in the sight of God. Do you pray for God to show you how you can save more so as to be able to give more? Do you pray for God to make you prosperous so you can sacrifice more?

Money is truly sacred when it is given to God. Giving to God can be holy worship, expressive of your longing and your love. God gave all that He had to give—His very Son. Do you give all that you have to give?

∞

Lord, fill me with the love and joy of giving.

You Are Important to God 33

It is very important to God that you understand how much He loves you. You are special to Him. He has holy plans for you. You are already quite different from the person you formerly were. Perhaps you have not fully realized how God has been working in your life.

No two of us are alike. You have a personality that is different from that of many others, and when you are filled with and led by the Holy Spirit, God can use you for some assignments for which no one else is fully prepared. You are important to God.

You are not yet all that God plans for you to be. God is not finished with His plans for your life. He has been patient with you because He loves you so much. He also is patient with you because He sees what you can be by His grace. God has important plans for you.

Hear His word: "'I know the plans I have for you,' declares the Lord, 'plans to prosper you and not to harm you, plans to give you hope and a future'" (Jer. 29:11). In the next two verses God adds, "'Then you will call upon me and come and pray to me, and I will listen to you. You will seek me and find me when you seek me with all your heart.'"

So not only are you important to God, but your prayer life also is important to God. He can use you only as He desires and plans to do when your prayer life is sufficient and adequate. You need to spend enough time in prayer, and the way you pray is also important to God.

Let me repeat His word to you in verse 13: "You will seek me and find me when you seek me with all your heart." A casual interest in God and His will is not enough for God to be able to use you greatly. You must be whole-souled. You must love Him with all your heart and be committed to Him with all your heart.

If you come to love Him more and more, if you learn to understand His will more clearly as you read His Word and walk more closely to Him, if you obey Him more carefully and more gladly each day, God will be able to fulfill His plans for you.

You are so important to God that it is important that you are always at your best for Him. He is eager to give you His best as soon as you learn to ask and receive more and more of His presence and power. God delights to become more and more real in your life. God is thrilled when you give Him more opportunities to use you.

Yes, you are very important to God. In fact, you are so important that He wants to help you become more like Him each day and more effective as His representative. It is urgent that you be at your best for Him. Expect Him to bless you. Plan the steps you will take to know Him better. Expect Him to make His love more real to you as you take time to be alone with Him.

May God use these brief meditations again and again to add burning coals to your soul's altar and cause you to blaze for Him. You are important to God.

Thank You, Lord, for loving me so personally.

Winds of Revival

During the last week of January 1970, Dr. Eugene Erny, former president of OMS International, and I, along with other missionary colleagues, were in a committee session in Wilmore, Kentucky, a small town where Asbury College and Asbury Theological Seminary are located. The college has approximately one thousand students. The seminary across the street has about nine hundred students.

While we were there the then newly appointed president of Asbury College, Dr. Dennis F. Kinlaw, heard that we were in town, and sent word asking us to come to his office after we had finished our committee business. When we arrived, he called in his dean, and these men opened their hearts to us and told us of their deep concern for the youth of America—the declining moral standards, the drug problem, and the repercussions of these things among the less spiritual elements of their student body.

They had a great desire that something be done to protect their students and to give them the highest level of spiritual nurture along with the highest academic education. We spent two hours together in discussion and prayer.

Just one week from that day there was a regular morning chapel service at the college. There was no speaker scheduled, so opportunities were given to students to testify. As the testimonies began, the sovereign hand of God moved with unusual power and blessing upon the student body. One after another, students rose to testify of Christ's closeness to them and to request special prayer for personal spiritual needs. By a sovereign act of God, deep Holy Spirit revival broke out in the midst of the chapel service.

This session, which began on February 3, 1970, continued nonstop for at least 144 hours. During most of this time the college chapel was crowded. It normally seats 1,200 people but, at times, many more were crowded in. All classes in the college were dismissed. Students from the seminary across the street also came into the services, and many found real blessing. When the news reached the people living in the town, a number of them began to come and sit in on the services, and many spiritual needs were met.

Students who received new spiritual victory called their parents and friends long distance and testified to what God had done for them. This so gripped many parents and friends that many of them drove hundreds of miles to be present for the services. Many who entered the services stayed for hours. Many stayed throughout the night, without leaving the auditorium.

News reached the radio and TV stations and quickly spread. One of the most well-known TV news telecasts in the United States, which broadcasts each night from coast to coast, asked permission to televise what God was doing at Asbury College. They gave five minutes of one of their evening telecasts to present a number of brief testimonies of students and then showed the entire crowded auditorium with more than 1,600 people singing the praises of God.

A person who was scheduled to have a cornea transplant operation came into the meetings and felt so impressed by the power of God that he rose and requested prayer for healing. Prayer was offered, and he was instantly healed. When he went to the hospital where the operation was scheduled, the hospital authorities, after an examination, told him that his eyes were perfect and that there was no need for surgery or treatment.

One young student who had been particularly rebellious was sitting in the back balcony of the auditorium. Gripped by the spirit of conviction, he came to the main floor and started forward for prayer. He was so seized by the need of his soul that he could not control himself and began to run down the aisle. He fell on his knees at the front of the chapel, calling upon God to have mercy on him.

Others who were sitting in the middle of the rows were also gripped by the urgency of their spiritual needs. Since people were sitting on both sides of them and it was difficult to get out, some climbed over the backs of the seats in front of them to hurry to the front to pray.

One young man who had become involved in a drug habit went out and flushed all his drugs down the toilet and then came forward to surrender his life to Christ. Another young man who had been involved in trafficking drugs was gripped by conviction of sin, confessed his need, and was completely delivered.

Students in Azusa Pacific University in California, hearing of what was happening, telephoned to request that a representative of the student body fly to California and share his or her testimony with them. Revival then spread to Azusa Pacific and also to Seattle Pacific University in the state of Washington! Revival also spread to a number of other Christian and secular college campuses. Students from a number of nearby campuses not only came and attended the services, but many were gripped by God and shared spontaneously in the praying and testifying.

The only complete record is in heaven, but within four months revival fire had spread to 130 different campuses, and at least 2,000 student teams had gone out by invitation to more than 2,000 churches, carrying torches of revival fire.

Although the revival is considered merely a psychological phenomenon by many skeptical people, Dr. Kinlaw told the press on the first Thursday that such movements of the Spirit of God have firm historical precedents in the life of the church universal and in the life of American colleges and universities. He underscored the fact that such happenings were not considered suspect in the early life of such schools as Dartmouth, Princeton, and Yale. There is available documentation of outstanding people in American history who have had conversion experiences in similar college awakenings.

Obviously, around-the-clock revival could not continue indefinitely. Yet many testified to spiritual renewal and blessing that came to them through this sovereign working of the Spirit of God. Many students gave witness to an abiding inner peace and transformation in their lives.

It was particularly thrilling to us that just one week after the president of the college had voiced his deep concern and shared this with us in prayer and conversation, God's mighty movement of revival began. How little we realize in the times when we sense our greatest need that the mighty answer of God to our earnest prayer may be very near!

The God who has worked so mightily in times past is working yet today. Anything that God has done for others He can, if it be His will, repeat today. The Spirit of God who at times has visited different parts of various nations can come again and can meet the needs of our churches and our people.

Let us in new faith claim the promises of God, for He is a covenant-keeping God, and nothing is too hard for Him. He has promised, "If my people, who are called by my name, will humble themselves and pray and seek my face and turn from their wicked ways, then will I hear from heaven and will forgive their sin and will heal their land" (2 Chron. 7:14). May it please God to visit us with a gracious revelation of His mighty power until our prayers of years are answered in days. To God be all the praise!

Lord, send revival to our campuses again.

Just for Jesus' Sake

We must do more for God. When we look at the sacrifice Jesus made for us and measure our lives in the light of His cross, nothing we have ever done for God seems adequate or significant. We are in eternal debt to Jesus; we owe all we are and all we have to Him.

If it were not for His grace, we would not be alive today. Without His grace, we would be without God and without hope. Without His mercy, so new every day, we would not have a place in His kingdom. If we had had only God's justice, we would already have been doomed. But we have had mercy after mercy, grace after grace, undeserved blessing after undeserved blessing. It is impossible for us to measure how much we owe to God.

But how little we have done for God! Almost everything we have ever done for God has brought some blessing to us. Again and again when we have thought we were doing something special for God, we were subconsciously aware that it would bring blessing to ourselves also. How often what we have claimed to do for God we have done in part because it was also being done for ourselves, for our family, for our church, for our organization.

It is not wrong to seek to do for God that which will also bring blessing, credit, or some reward to us. But we need to watch our motives. Again and again we need to reexamine our hearts to make sure we are really doing our service out of love for God.

God specially rewards us for what we do for Him in secret. That is one reason why prayer will bring such great rewards in eternity. We must do more that is hidden and unknown but is a real love offering for God. What can you do for Jesus without having others find out? What can you do to bring blessing to others and yet remain unseen yourself? How long has it been since you have really been extravagant in your service to God and yet delighted that no one knew about it?

Do you know the joy of giving until it hurts and not letting anyone find out about it? Do you know the joy of asking God for some special task that you can do, and then getting an opportunity known only to Him? Oh, my Christian friends, we must do more, we must do so much more out of pure joy in Him, out of pure love for Him, out of extravagant love for Him.

Have you ever asked God to give you someone to love for Him? He has people He can love through you. They may have very unattractive dispositions. It may be that you would prefer to show your love to almost anyone else. There may be a real hidden cost to you if you are extravagant in your love to them.

Perhaps they have wronged you or slandered you. Perhaps they naturally irritate you and have such a different disposition from yours that they are a constant trial to you. Perhaps it almost disturbs your communion with God to even think about them. What can you do to lavish a special Christlike love on them? Are they your biggest hindrance in your walk with God? Then can you ask God to let you do some hidden loving service for them? Is there anyone to whom you should show the kindness of Christ, the sympathy of Christ, the forgiveness of Christ today (see 2 Sam. 9:3)?

Oh, we must do more to love others for God. Not for our own sakes, not for the benefit we will receive, not because we enjoy being near them, but because we want to love them for Jesus' sake. Love them with the love Jesus had when He healed the ear of the one who was abusing Him. Love them with the love Jesus had when He forgave those who crucified Him. Love them with a costly, fragrant, Christlike love.

Ask God to whom you can show a truly Christlike love today. We must do more than love those who love us. We must do more than pray for those who are dear to us. We must do more for the totally undeserving and the unlovely because of pure love of Jesus—just because we love Him so.

These are the things that are really Christian. These are the love offerings that are fragrant, pleasing sacrifices in the sight of God. These are the things that draw us closer to God than we have ever been before. These are the things that will give us a joy too deep for words. We are so ready to do things that others will know about. Let us do more for Jesus alone, just out of love for Him, just out of grateful thanks to Him.

There is someone near you who has never understood the love of Jesus. Ask God to show you how you can make it real to that person. There is someone who has never really known a Christlike, unselfish love. Do something costly—not necessarily in money, but costly in love. Invest love without hoping for returns—just out of love for Jesus. Pray much first; ask God to show you how to do it. Ask God to prepare the way. Ask God to prepare you so that your sacrifice may be hidden and only He will see and know about it.

In the meantime, start doing more for Jesus today. Smile at some children as you lovingly pray for them in secret in your heart. Ask God to help them feel your love. Ask God whom you can bless today. As you walk down the street, ask God how you can be Christlike to someone today. As you kneel in silence in your home, ask God to give His love to someone through you today.

Don't wait. Do it now. Ask God what you can do now. Tell Jesus how much you love Him now. Ask Him to help you do more for Him than ever before—just for Him, just for your love for Him, just for His sake. Oh, the joy that is waiting for you! Oh, the precious revelation of His love that is awaiting you when you do more for Him, just for Him!

∞

Lord, give me things to do "just for You" today.

Work in the Spirit

If one tenth of the work done in the name of Christ were done in the power and anointing of the Holy Spirit, this world would be turned upside down for God! It is significant that in John's letters to the churches found in Revelation 2 and 3 this phrase repeatedly occurs: "I know your deeds." The church has always been known for its activities. The church that does not labor will soon die. The minister who does not bend every energy to fulfill his sacred calling is not worthy of the name of Christ.

Satan is not necessarily opposed to all Christian work! He cares little about how zealously we busy ourselves in good things unless we work in the power of the Holy Spirit. He is pleased if we work so hard and so long that we begin to fret and worry. He is happy if we undertake more work than we can permeate with prayer. He does not seriously oppose every Christian who is a tireless worker—so long as he or she works only in human energy and is not empowered and anointed by the Spirit of God.

It is possible to have the witness of the Spirit that you are a child of God and yet undertake most of your activities in your human strength and wisdom rather than with the power and wisdom of the Holy Spirit. It is possible to be filled with the Spirit and yet do things in your own strength rather than in the power of the Holy Spirit. The temptation is constantly present to depend on human logic rather than on the guidance of the Holy Spirit, to "get along" depending on past experience and blessing rather than seeking and obtaining constant new anointing and the fresh outpouring of God's Spirit upon you.

The New Testament standard of spiritual life consists of a crisis experience that involves being crucified with Christ, purified by faith, and filled with the Spirit, followed by repeated outpourings, anointings, and fillings with the Holy Spirit. There must come a time in your experience when you enter the life of the Spirit, but you need also to appropriate new power, new blessing, new anointing, and new help for your life and service repeatedly.

The reason the church of the apostles was so invincible, so victorious, and so fruitful was that it was a church that experienced a crisis cleansing and filling with the Spirit on the Day of Pentecost. Then followed definite new infillings of the Spirit as emergencies arose and as the needs of their work demanded.

The central fact of their experience was not the outward manifestations of wind, fire, and languages; the central fact was that their lives were pure and powerful (Acts 15:8–9). If you are not filled with purity and power, you are not Spirit-filled, no matter what experiences you may claim to have had.

If you have entered into life in the Spirit, you have the right to appropriate a new anointing or filling of the Spirit to prepare you and strengthen you for every new responsibility, every new undertaking for Christ. The anointing is an abiding anointing if the Holy Spirit abides in you (1 John 2:27), for the anointing is really the presence of the Anointer. If He abides in you, you have a right to ask Him repeatedly to perform the work of His office by anointing you afresh.

May God save us from the frustration of a life too busy to be anointed! May He save us from fruitless endeavors that demonstrate that we failed to live and work in the fullness of the Spirit! The omnipotent God who spoke worlds into existence wants to work through us. The mighty power that raised Jesus from the dead has been given to us to energize our ministry. This is the dispensation of the Holy Spirit.

The hour has come for God to demonstrate His mighty power anew in your life and mine, in your ministry and mine. Let us humble ourselves at the Cross until we experience anew the New Testament norm for life and ministry. You can see the supernatural power of God at work if you will meet God's conditions. You can have a changed life and a changed ministry. Obey, believe, receive!

Lord, may I live and serve today with the fresh presence and power of the Holy Spirit.

Are You Partially Christian?

"I know your deeds, that you are neither cold nor hot. I wish you were either one or the other!" (Rev. 3:15).

It is because we have been only partially Christian that the world has become almost wholly pagan. Our partially Christian church is responsible for the almost universally Christless state of the world. This indictment is tragically true of the Christian church in every land. Is it true of your church? Is it true of you? Not only are there large areas of our lives untouched by Christ, but that part of our life that we think is most Christian—our spiritual life—is tragically mediocre, incomplete, and imperfect. We are only partially Christian.

A partial Christian is largely useless to himself, to the world, and to God. He has divided interests and a divided heart. He owes allegiance to many masters. His is an impossible position. And yet there are millions of Christians filling our churches who only partially belong to Christ. They are only mildly interested in the things of God and of the church.

In the lives of millions the self is reigning on the throne of their hearts. Christ is tolerated and honored as a guest, but no more than that. In no sense are their hearts His throne or His home. His will is largely unobeyed, His interests are largely neglected, and His desires are largely disregarded. Christ is only a spiritual figurehead in their lives. Nominally He is their Lord; practically and actually He is only a casual acquaintance. Is this a true picture of you?

A partial Christian is a worldly Christian. He is charmed more by the world than by the spiritual claims of Christ. He has the ideals of the world, the outlook of the world, the attitude of the world. He thinks as the world thinks; he lives much as the world lives. His methods are those of the world.

1. He is quite comfortable with the songs, the music, the literature, the jokes, and the television menu.

2. He is almost more comfortable with average unsaved people than he is with deeply spiritual people.

3. He is more comfortable to leave the television on for hours than to spend a whole hour with Jesus, reading His Word, and praying. He has never learned to intercede, to use prayer lists, or to prevail in prayer for national or world needs.

Christ came to do a complete work, a perfect work. He came not merely to diminish the works of the devil but to destroy them (1 John 3:8). "Therefore he is able to save completely those who come to God through him" (Heb. 7:25). He gives new desires, new longings, new interests, new vision, new strength, and new victory. He came to make us "more than conquerors" (Rom. 8:37). He came to give us spiritual life "to the full" (John 10:10).

The only life that has power to attract others to Christ is the life that is totally and wholeheartedly committed to Him. Only when Christ is Lord of everything in our lives does the world sit up and take notice. A defeated Christian, a powerless Christian, a Christian living a subnormal Christian life is often worse than useless. He is a dead weight to the cause of Christ. He is a hindrance to Christ and to His church.

A partial Christian disappoints and dishonors Christ. Only an out-and-out Christian, only a life absolutely and constantly surrendered to God, a life of abounding spiritual victory makes an unsaved person hungry to know Christ. Only such a person can become the seed of revival in a lifeless community or church.

Are you a partial Christian? You can be changed! There is just one way for the partial Christian to become a dynamic, radiant, victorious Christian. It is the way that leads to a cross. Your sinful self-centeredness must be crucified. Your self must be slain. When self dies, the power of the world dies, recurring defeat is changed into victory, Christ ascends the throne, and fruitfulness and victory fill one's life.

Let us not hold back. Christ already means much to us. Shall we not seek His face until He means everything to us, until He is in reality our All-in-All? God and the world are waiting for us to become out-and-out Christians. God and the world are waiting for us to become totally Christlike. God forbid that we be spiritually cold. God forbid that we be only lukewarm. Let us be ablaze for God, aglow with the fire of His Holy Spirit.

The Shekinah glory can descend upon the church once more. The holy fire can descend from heaven once more and rest upon each one of us (Acts 2:3). We may be totally unconscious of it, as Moses the man of God was (Ex. 34:29), but the world will know the difference. We too will know that a new day has dawned in our experience and in our work.

It is not for spectacular signs and manifestations that I plead. It is the silent, sacred, holy, and irresistible power of God that must possess our lives till we are strongest where we were once weakest. Then we will be "more than conquerors" where we were once defeated. Then the hidden beauty and glory of God will rest upon us—the spirit of grace and glory.

Oh, my friends, let us not be satisfied with anything less. Full surrender is the will of God. Revival fires can burn again. The miracle of God can come again. Tides of salvation can sweep over our lands again. Our churches can become centers of life and power and unity and love again. The Shekinah glory can descend on each one of us again when all partial things are cast aside, when all half-heartedness and indifference are purged from our lives, and when Christ and His kingdom are first in our hearts and first in our lives. O Spirit of the living God, come upon us anew today!

Lord, make me a total Christian, Christlike in everything!!

Be Thankful
and Bless His Name

Do we really bless God by our thankfulness? David wrote, "Enter his gates with thanksgiving and his courts with praise; give thanks to him and praise his name" (Ps. 100:4).

Every time we leave our home to go to church, we ought to begin to thank God for the privilege of worshiping and serving Him. We should enter church doors with our heads up, with a Christian smile of peace on our faces, and with a prayer of praise ascending from our hearts. How our services, our singing, and our praying would be transformed if we really had praising hearts!

God's blessing begins to show on your countenance when you bless His name in your heart. Every time you see a long-faced Christian, ask God to help you show Christ's joy. God not only wants to touch our hearts with glory, He also wants to manifest it in our attitudes, our words, and our facial expressions.

How rebuked I have felt at times when people have told me that my face showed that I was not happy. It is human to be weary, discouraged, and perplexed; it is Christian to have joy unspeakable and full of glory, to always triumph in Christ. The Christian should be known for his overcoming life and overflowing thankful heart in the midst of all circumstances.

How sacred and wonderful it is that our thankfulness to God brings joy to His heart! He is not a cold, passive "Eternal One." He is merciful love; He is our heavenly Father. If we appreciate the love shown to us, how much more must God value our love for Him. If a human father is happy when his children thank him, how much more must the infinite heart of our heavenly Father rejoice with a holy joy when we express our love and thankfulness to Him.

Have we grieved God's heart of love by our carelessness and forgetting to thank Him? Jesus asked, "Where are the nine?" when only one out of ten who were healed returned to give thanks. God is pouring His blessings upon our lives. Every day He answers many expressed or unexpressed prayers that were on our hearts. Do we really spend time with Him in just assuring Him of our love, our gratitude, or our joy in Him?

We are very quick to ask; our mouths are filled with petitions; our prayers are long with asking. May God help us to spend just as long a time worshiping Him, thanking Him, and rejoicing in Him with a holy, quiet joy, resting in His love. If the heart of a mother rejoices when her baby looks up into her face and smiles, if the heart of a father is thrilled when his sons and daughters tell him how much they appreciate his care for them, ought we not often look up into God's face and smile? Ought we not take time to kneel in His presence just to thank Him again and again?

Days of thanksgiving have been set aside by churches, organizations, and even nations. For us as true Christians, every day should be a day of thanksgiving. We owe much to our parents, our pastors, our friends, and others. Let us thank them for all they mean to us and all they do for us. But let us resolve to spend some time each day just thanking, adoring, and worshiping our wonderful Savior.

Lord, help me show my thankfulness.

We Must Have Unity

We must have unity if we want to see real revival. We must have unity if we want to see spiritual growth. We must have unity if we want to see a large ingathering of souls! Unity is imperative if we want to see mighty answers to prayer, if we want to see spiritual radiance, and if we want to see God's glory manifested.

Spiritual unity is not a delicacy at the Lord's table; it is not a luxury, available from the storehouse of heaven. Spiritual unity is essential to daily spiritual living. In godly group life there is no alternative to unity. Neither the group nor the individual within the group can become all that God desires unless they are doing all within their power to secure and maintain spiritual unity.

We need spiritual unity everywhere. We must have it in our Sunday schools among all the teachers and officers. We must have it in our churches among the members of the congregation, among the church officials, between pastor and people. We must have it in our Christian institutions—in our schools, our publishing organizations, and our hospitals. But perhaps most fundamentally of all, we must have unity in our homes.

The home is central to spiritual unity. He who speaks critically in public usually speaks even more critically at home. He who seeks to domineer in public has the habit of wanting his or her own way at home. The person who causes friction in public usually sulks at home, pouts at home, or makes wounds at home by sarcastic and cutting remarks. The person who fills the ears of the public with gossip and criticism usually says even more to the people within the home. She who poisons the thoughts of the neighbors or the church usually fills her own home with poisoned air from her unsanctified mouth.

One of the greatest cures for disunity is prayer. Don't discuss the weakness of a brother until you have prayed long and humbly for that brother, thanking God first for all the good in him. Don't air your differences in public until you have sought to spend time together with that brother in earnest and protracted prayer. Don't pray at your brother and think you are praying with your brother. Prayer unites, prayer removes difficulties, prayer melts together. Minutes spent together in prayer may not do this, but hours spent together will, especially when these are spent together in some quiet place alone. Don't pray only over your difficulty—pray over many things together, until your hearts become one. Unity grows in the atmosphere of prayer.

But there is another step that will perhaps do more than all else to restore unity, especially when this step is taken in a spirit of humble prayer. There is no magic way to unity, but there is a miracle way—the way commended by Christ Himself. "If you are offering your gift at the altar and there remember that your brother has something against you, leave your gift there in front of the altar. First go and be reconciled to your brother; then come and offer your gift" (Matt. 5:23–24). No one can say he has done his part to restore unity until he has gone humbly to his brother, taking the path of meekly asking for forgiveness.

Christ does not raise the question of who is to blame. Assigning blame is a very difficult and dangerous occupation. Forget for the moment about all you feel and think you know. Does your brother hold something against you? Then your obligation is clear: You must take the initiative and go to him, asking his forgiveness. "But," you say, "I am utterly innocent." Christ does not raise the question of innocence or guilt. He says if there is disunity, go to your brother and ask for forgiveness. Don't go trying first to justify your-self and then adding, "Now if you feel I have done anything against you, please forgive me." This is the way of self-defense; it is not the way to seek forgiveness. Leave your reasons behind; go with a bro-ken spirit, broken over the tragedy of disunity, and, humbling your-self, ask sincerely for forgiveness.

You answer, "But it won't work; it will make things worse." How do you know until you have obeyed Christ's command? If you keep remembering that there is a difference between you, the command is clear—"Go." But don't go until your own heart has been broken and melted in the Lord's presence. Don't go until God has baptized you with the spirit of Calvary's love. Go to the Cross first, then go to your brother.

Unity costs, but it is worth all it costs. There is no alternative to unity if you want God's full blessing. There is no shortcut to God's favor and His miracle working. There is no alternative to unity, and there may be no alternative to your taking the costly, self-effacing way that Christ has outlined. Perhaps God is waiting for you to go to your brother.

∞

Lord, what can I do to increase unity?

Do You Have Eyes That See?

As Jesus and His disciples were returning from Judea, they passed through Samaria on their way to Galilee. Jesus was weary and thirsty, and He sat down by the well of Sychar. Then when he saw a Samaritan woman coming to draw water, he recognized that she had spiritual needs and that she was approachable (see John 4:1–34).

When the disciples arrived back from the town market they saw the Samaritan woman but not her need. They were surprised that Jesus was talking with her. They had good eyes, but they failed to see what Jesus saw. They did not see her empty heart and disappointment. She had been battered by life. She had been deceived by people. She had tried marriage five times, and each time she had been let down. She was now grasping at a straw and was living with a sixth man whom she wasn't even married to.

Not one of the disciples saw in her a prospective sister in Christ. Not one of them saw in her the key person for a mighty revival in Sychar. Probably not even one of the disciples had prayed for this village. Probably not one of them longed for God to open up Samaria to the Gospel or for God to guide the disciples to the place where Jesus would begin a Samaritan ministry. They had eyes, but they did not see. Why?

They did not understand the message of their Scriptures. They did not remember God's promise to Abraham, God's exhortations in the Psalms, or the words of the prophets. They did not remember the message the angels proclaimed when Jesus was born. They did not realize that God loved the whole world and sent Jesus to bless the whole world.

They had been chosen to represent Jesus and had been sent to various villages to prepare the way of the Lord. But they did not see the people as Jesus saw them. Once when they saw children surrounding Jesus, they felt that this was a bother and that children should not waste Jesus' time. But Jesus said, "Let the children gather around me. They can enjoy the blessings of salvation and My love, too" (Matt. 19:14).

The Canaanite woman with a demon-possessed daughter cried desperately for Jesus' help. The disciples did not see the mother's love or hear the deep cry of her heart. They said, "Send her away. She makes too much noise." But Jesus saw a woman of great faith, and so He delivered her daughter. Her story is still told around the world today (see Mark 7:24–30).

What do you see as you read your Bible? Do you see truth that you can apply to your own life? What do you see as you read your newspaper or watch TV news? Do you see one more sickening example of human sin to which you want to shut your eyes so that it doesn't bother you or haunt you? Or do you see these events as urgent prayer requests calling you to intercede for the people and the families involved in these tragedies?

Jesus told of the priest and the Levite who saw a man who had been beaten by robbers and had been left half dead on the road to Jericho (Luke 10:25–37). They quickly avoided the scene; they avoided involvement. After all, it was no problem of theirs. Or was it? When a family in our church or our community has problems, are we too unconcerned and too busy to get involved? After all, we think, these are not our problems. Or are they? God surely does not expect us to do anything. Or does He?

Do we have eyes to see the people who need us? Do we have ears to hear the cry of people we could help if we would? Do we have eyes to look for opportunities to let our light shine and to demonstrate our love? In John 4 Jesus said to His disciples, in effect: You are my followers, but you don't have eyes to see. You see people without seeing the opportunities to represent Me to them. You don't see the people who need your help. You don't recognize the opportunities to share My love with others. Lift up your eyes and look! (see John 4:35).

Could it be that one day Jesus will say to you and me, "I was hungry and you gave me nothing to eat. . . . I was a stranger and you did not invite me in, I needed clothes and you did not clothe me, I was sick and in prison and you did not look after me" (Matt. 25:42–43). Could it be that we will one day reply, "Lord, when did this happen?" Will we one day say, "Lord, I did not realize that You were waiting for me. I did not see You standing by the needy. I could have prayed so many times but my eyes were blinded. I forgot Your will for my life."

Lord, help me to do more than just look. Give me eyes that see.

This Experience Is for You

There is an experience of victory available to every Christian whereby he or she can praise God, saying with Paul, "But thanks be to God, who always leads us in triumphal procession in Christ" (2 Cor. 2:14). There is a personal experience available for you so that you can say with Paul, "I have been crucified with Christ and I no longer live, but Christ lives in me" (Gal. 2:20). There is an experience through which you can be holy in all you do (1 Peter 1:15). Having purified yourself by obeying the truth, you have sincere love for your brothers and love each other deeply, from the heart (1 Peter 1:22). There is an experience in which you can be clothed with power from on high (Luke 24:49), be filled with the Spirit (Eph. 5:18), live in the Spirit, and continually manifest the fruit of the Spirit (Gal. 5:22–23).

It is the strategy of Satan to make you believe that the victorious, Spirit-filled, holy life that always overcomes was for God's special saints of a previous age or generation. Perhaps he tells you it is only for a few spiritually gifted people but not for you. You know your weaknesses too well; you know your past failures too well. You are very conscious of defeats, and you are not really expecting a different spiritual experience in the near future.

Praise God, there is in Scripture the promise and picture of a life of spiritual victory and power. It is described in various biblical terms. It is the life of victory, the crucified life, the Spirit-filled life, the sanctified life, the holy life, the empowered life, the overcoming life. It is described as a life of spiritual freedom, spiritual rest, and perfect love. It is an experience of spiritual circumcision, of death to the carnal self, of resurrection power, of being baptized with the Holy Spirit and fire, of cleansing by the precious blood of Christ.

Great men of God have used various nonbiblical terms to describe this wonderful experience. It has been called the deeper life, the higher life, the victorious life, the life of absolute surrender, the quiet life, the life of Christian perfection, the life on the higher plane, the radiant life, the life of power. It matters little what you call it; what really matters is that you know it as a personal, present experience of your own.

Perhaps you disagree with the explanations and theories of others concerning this experience, but the question is this: Does your theory work in your own life? Are you now living in constant victory, purity, and power? If your theory does not work for you today, either you have the wrong theory or else you have the right theory but have failed to meet God's conditions. Either one of these is tragic.

Perhaps you have been prejudiced by the carnal, unsanctified living of someone who claimed to possess this experience but failed to show it in daily living, or by the unscriptural claims or extravagant language of others. Perhaps you have been taught that you must expect defeat as long as you are in this world. It may be that the only ones who have described this experience to you have insisted that everyone had to have the same kind of emotional experience, outward sign, "gift," or "evidence." They claimed you needed this in order to know you were Spirit-filled. Such people may be sincere, but they have not understood the full message of Scripture.

The Holy Spirit does not need any gift or sign to prove His presence. He is Himself the Witness to your soul. There is no spiritual gift or manifestation that cannot be counterfeited or misused.

There is no one gift of the Spirit that proves a life of victory. The Holy Spirit divides His gifts individually as He sees fit, not in accordance with our demands. The main proof of a Spirit-filled life is the presence of the Holy Spirit Himself in all His fullness within the heart of the believer, giving His constant rest, victory, love, and power. It is an invisible but wonderfully knowable experience in the believer's inner nature that is soon manifest in his or her outer life.

The Spirit-filled person will have streams of living water flowing from within and blessing all around (John 7:38–39). The Spirit-filled person will have the love of God poured out in his heart by the Holy Spirit (Rom. 5:5), and this love will manifest itself in the beautiful graces and the absence of carnal manifestations as shown in 1 Corinthians 13.

The proof of a life of victory is victory—constant victory through Christ. The proof of sanctification is sanctified living. The proof of being baptized with the Holy Spirit and fire is the constant empowering for daily living—not for spectacular miracles or occasional signs and wonders—but the power to live victoriously over defeats, to live humbly, lovingly, and radiantly in every situation in life.

Is this the experience you hunger for? Is not this the experience clearly portrayed in Scripture from many different angles? The Holy Spirit teaches us that no one Bible term or illustration is adequate to describe this glorious experience. By divine inspiration a full range of descriptive terms have been given to us. You will never rightly understand or explain this precious and most wonderfully real experience of God's grace unless you take into account all that the Bible says, the entire Scripture.

Just as the new birth is described in many ways and by many terms in Scripture, so is the life of victory and holiness. Just as no human language is adequate to describe the wonders and joy of the forgiveness of sins, so no human language is adequate to describe the wonders and glory of the fullness of the Spirit—the sanctification the disciples still needed and for which Christ prayed in John 17. The promise is for you as much as for them (Acts 2:39). You can experience as complete a cleansing of heart and as radiant and powerful a daily spiritual living as they did. God is no respecter of persons or times. This is still the dispensation of the Holy Spirit.

The great need of the church today is for men and women, pastors and laymen, the youth and the aged, to be filled with the Spirit, to be clothed from on high with the power of the Holy Spirit, to live the life of daily, constant sanctified love, heart rest, and spiritual victory. The church can be set ablaze for God only when its members once more experience the reality of that for which Christ died and the Spirit was sent. "And so Jesus also suffered outside the city gate to make the people holy through his own blood" (Heb. 13:12).

When Jesus prayed, "Sanctify them by the truth; your word is truth," He prayed for you (John 17:17, 20). "I am going to send you what my Father has promised" (Luke 24:49). "The promise is for you . . . and . . . for all whom the Lord our God will call" (Acts 2:39). "If you then, though you are evil, know how to give good gifts to your children, how much more will your Father in heaven give the Holy Spirit to those who ask him!" (Luke 11:13).

The promise, said Peter, is for you. This experience is for you. Resurrection power and life are for you. The fullness of the Spirit is for you. The victorious life is for you. All of God's provision and power are available for you. The Holy Spirit is here today for you. He is waiting to do within your heart and life all that you long for and all that you need.

First, you must know that your sins are all forgiven and that you are a child of God. Then you must make a total surrender of yourself to God as a living sacrifice, giving up your own will and accepting His will for all your days and all your ways, and you must trust Him with a childlike trust to fulfill His promise (see Acts 26:18).

The Scripture's descriptions of this experience are not unattainable ideals. They are not there to make you hungry and leave you unsatisfied. God's Word means what it says. This promise, this experience is for you.

∞

Lord, may I experience all Your grace has provided for me.

Resurrection Power
for You Today

   You should be as triumphant over sin as Christ was over death. The Bible repeatedly associates Christ's death and resurrection with what should be the normal Christian victory over spiritual death and the normal spiritual triumph in abundance of life. The Christian is to be a person crucified with Christ and raised with Christ in a new life of spiritual power and victory.

   Paul realized that there was great danger that many Christians would not experience this fullness of resurrection power and would fail to realize the standard of Christian life to which God calls each of us. Therefore, he ceaselessly prayed for the Christians that the eyes of their heart would be enlightened so they would "know ... his incomparably great power for [those] who believe. That power is like the working of his mighty strength, which he exerted in Christ when he raised him from the dead and seated him at his right hand in the heavenly realms" (Eph. 1:18–20; see also Eph. 2:6; Col. 3:1–10).

   Do you understand Christ's resurrection power as primarily a theory of what happened for you two thousand years ago? Is it only nominal in your life today? Or is it primarily a glorious reality in your everyday life? Are you only glorifying and praising God for what His resurrection power did for you at the resurrection of

Christ, or are you daily rejoicing in the "incomparable" greatness of present resurrection power that gives you present triumph over the world, the flesh, and the Devil? Are you triumphing in a present-tense resurrection experience?

Satan's great desire is to get Christians to put off to some future date the experience and life God wants us to enjoy today. Satan wants to make us content to be weak and powerless when God's standard is for the power of the Holy Spirit to remain in us now. Satan wants us to excuse ourselves as being "weak human beings" when God wants us here and now to be children of God, purifying ourselves even as God Himself is pure (1 John 3:2–10). Satan wants us to be carnal Christians walking in the flesh instead of victorious believers walking in the Spirit (Gal. 5:16), carnally minded instead of spiritually minded, controlled by the flesh instead of controlled by the Spirit (Rom. 8:6–8).

God wants us to realize that He sent His Son to condemn all sinful defeats so that God's righteousness will not merely be our theoretical goal but that it will be fulfilled in us as we walk in the Spirit (Rom. 8:3–5). It is the Spirit's role to fulfill in us what Christ provided for us.

Paul testified that this resurrection power worked mightily in his own life (Eph. 3:20; Col. 1:29) and that he wanted his converts also to have their faith grounded in this mighty power of the Holy Spirit (1 Cor. 2:4–5). Quoting Isaiah 64:4, he pointed out a few verses later, "'No eye has seen, no ear has heard, no mind has conceived what God has prepared for those who love him,' but God has revealed it to us by his Spirit" (vv. 9–10). Satan tries to mislead people to think that this is a description of heaven. Paul says it is a description of what God wants to do for us here. But he adds that the natural man does not understand this (v. 14), and this was why the Corinthian Christians were failing—they were living carnal lives on the natural human plane (3:1–4).

Resurrection power is overcoming power available to every Christian every day of his life. Triumph should be the normal everyday experience of every Christian. Fellow believer, your eye has never seen and it has never begun to enter your mind what a wonderfully triumphant experience of God's grace and power He wants you to enjoy daily.

Resurrection power for the Christian is not primarily spectacular power to *do*, it is God's amazing power to enable you to *be*. God wants your life to be a demonstration of the very same power of the Holy Spirit that raised Christ from the dead. He doesn't want your life to manifest spiritual defeat and to carry about the smell of death; He wants your life to manifest abundance of life, victory, and glory—to manifest the sweet fragrance and aroma of Christ wherever you go (2 Cor. 2:14–15). He wants your daily life to be a living demonstration of the world's greatest miracle—resurrection power.

Lord, help me live in resurrection power today.

Guilty of Not Getting Involved!

43

God holds people responsible for getting involved in the needs of others. To see a need that you can fill when you are present or available is often God's opportunity and assignment for you to act. To avoid involvement is not only not being a neighbor, as Jesus encouraged us to be, but it is also an omission for which we will be held personally accountable by God.

The fact that it is inconvenient may not make you excusable in God's sight. There are almost always other things you can do to avoid involvement, but that may not clear you before God. "Anyone, then, who knows the good he ought to do and doesn't do it, sins" (James 4:17). Sins of omission can make you guilty before God.

Proverbs 24:11–12 gives us very clear instruction: "Rescue those being led away to death; hold back those staggering toward slaughter. If you say, 'But we knew nothing about this,' does not he who weighs the heart perceive it? Does not he who guards your life know it? Will he not repay each person according to what he has done?" Some people are ignorant of a situation because they close their eyes. Some have avoided attending a missionary service for fear they might get involved. Some avoid evangelistic meetings for fear

God might convict them of their sins. This makes them doubly guilty before God.

God is full of compassion (Ps. 116:5). He is great in compassion (51:1). He has compassion on all He has made (145:9). As a father has compassion on his children, so the Lord has compassion on you (103:13). This is why God is so pleased whenever you give to missions and to those in need. It pleases God greatly when you try to find how you can help and when you immediately and repeatedly pray for those in need. He wants you to be a person of compassion.

God expects every Christian today to carry a prayer burden for missions. He expects every pastor to help his people receive such a prayer burden. Any believer who avoids becoming involved in missionary need becomes guilty before God. God sends missionaries back to their homeland to help the Christians get more of a vision and become more involved. Any pastor who fails to encourage his people to get involved is a grief to God's loving heart and robs God's people of the blessing and revival God longs to give.

It has been nearly two thousand years since Jesus died for the whole world. But much of the world has not yet had a clear gospel invitation. The church is collectively guilty before God, and this can cause the church to be less blessed by God. God has been deeply grieved and pained by the failure of His church. God wants us to open our hearts to the need of the world, and there is no greater need than the need of salvation.

We are a better informed generation of Christians than any previous generation; so we are more responsible than all who preceded us. God wants us to have compassion as He has compassion. God wants us to share the gospel light with those who have not yet received it. God wants us to share with others the spiritual blessings that He has lavished on us.

Do we dare to use the excuse of Proverbs 24:12 and say we did not know the need of the millions who have never heard? If we do not know their needs, it is because we have not exposed ourselves to their needs. We know there are several billion unsaved and often largely unreached remaining in our world. We know that there are many worthy international missionary organizations engaged in aggressive evangelism—many in several parts of the world.

The question is, Do we try to expose ourselves to the need of the world, or do we choose to ignore it? Are we investing our money generously to aid the worldwide evangelization being done by worthy, respected, and aggressively evangelistic people and organizations? Do we use daily prayer lists to guide our personal intercession and make sure that we pray earnestly for several nations or regions of the world and several worthy missionary organizations every day?

We rejoice in the privilege of prayer fellowship with God. But often that is about the only kind of prayer we pray—the prayer of fellowship with God. The Bible emphasizes intercession for others. God has called us to be His royal priesthood (1 Peter 2:9). The main responsibility of a priest is not to pray for himself but to pray for others. Of course, he must himself keep close to God and right with God. But a priest has a responsibility to pray for others. If God calls us His priests, He is holding us responsible to pray for those about us and to pray for our needy world. A brief time of personal fellowship with God is necessary to our spiritual life. God forgive us if we omit that. But that alone does not completely satisfy the heart of God. We are responsible to have a daily detailed and effective prayer life for others.

One day you and I will stand before Christ as He sits on His judgment throne (2 Cor. 5:10) and as He judges us and rewards us for how we invested our love, our prayer, and our money after we were saved by His grace (1 Cor. 3:11–15). Will our tears then be tears of joy because at last we are face to face with the Lord we have loved and served so faithfully? Or will our tears be tears of shame because we neglected our opportunities and responsibilities in prayer, disappointed the loving heart of Jesus, and failed to be the priests of God He saved us to be?

∞

Lord, make me a priest today through my prayer.

"Why Are You Sleeping? Get up and Pray"

For three years Christ had taught and trained His disciples. For three years He had let them share His ministry, His miracle-working power, His comfort, His encouragement, and His blessing. Now He had come to the hour of His agony and travail, and He took His disciples with Him to Gethsemane, going a little distance farther with His chosen few. In the midnight hour of prayer agony He longed for their prayer-fellowship, but they soon fell asleep.

The Son of God was wrestling with the burden of the world's sin—but the disciples slept. He prayed until His heart was crushed with the weight of their sin—but the disciples slept. He prayed until His sweat became like great drops of blood falling down on the ground—but they slept on. One of their own number had become a traitor and was even now doing his devilish worst—but they slept on.

Satan was planning to defeat God's plan of redemption, to damn the sin-fettered world—but the disciples slept on. It was the hour of the world's greatest crisis; the disciples were needed, they were given a privilege angels would long to have shared—but the disciples slept. It was the greatest opportunity they had ever had to prove their love for Christ—but they slept on. All heaven and hell were watching to see what they would do. Three times Jesus came and awakened them.

Do you feel like calling them ungrateful, unsympathetic, indifferent, lazy disciples? unworthy, unspiritual? Wait! Beware lest in condemning them you condemn yourself! Today, as then, angelic beings hover near you. Elect angels are witnesses of your own faithfulness or carelessness (see 1 Tim. 5:21; cf. Eccl. 5:6).

For years Christ has been training you. He has blessed you, supplying your material, physical, and spiritual needs. He has guided you step by step. His angels have protected you. He has been your constant help; He has never failed you. For years He has been preparing you and training you—but will His angel, ever at your side, report that spiritually you are still asleep?

Once more the world, your land, your friends are in sorrow and in need. Once more it is a crisis hour. Mighty forces, seen and unseen, are engaged in a crucial conflict. Decisions taken today may lead whole nations to war or to peace. Decisions taken today may lead to wider doors of gospel opportunity or to restrictions on the people of God. Decisions taken today may lead your friends and neighbors to Christ and salvation or away from Christ to eternal night. The destiny of many is in the balance—but are you spiritually asleep?

Spiritual leaders and organizations are toiling night and day for revival. Some are fasting and praying that multitudes may turn to God. Never have so many hearts been open to the Gospel. Never have we had such opportunity because of the extraordinary means of literature, radio, TV, and other aids at our disposal. Now, as never before, it is possible to influence a generation for God.

Revival is promised in the Word; touches of revival are blessing many nations. This is God's hour. This is when your effort can count the most for God. This is the hour of God-given opportunity for you. Others are dedicating their all for God and human souls. Others are praying, interceding with tears and fasting, pleading and agonizing for souls. Are you still asleep?

Do not condemn Peter, James, and John for their neglect. Is not yours a greater neglect? Do not despise those sleeping disciples if you, too, are equally asleep! Christ's voice echoing down the centuries speaks to you today: "WHY ARE YOU SLEEPING? . . . GET UP AND PRAY" (Luke 22:46).

Lord, don't let me sleep on when You are waiting for my prayer.

When Revival Came in India

Some years ago while editing *Revival* magazine, I received a letter, which read in part as follows:

At one of the conferences we saw God coming down in an unusual way. There were about 600 delegates from different places and about 2,000 people who came from the neighborhood. For the first two days the meetings were just ordinary. So the Lord gave a great burden for the meetings.

All the hundreds of delegates decided to go without breakfast the last day. At four-thirty in the morning I got up with another brother to pray. He is a humble, unlearned man. We were on our knees for an hour and a half and the Lord revealed to this brother that He was going to visit the people and we praised Him in advance.

We started the meeting at 7:00 a.m. The Lord guided in the devotional talks on "The God who answers by fire is God." The enemy fought real hard during the meeting. But the enemy could not hinder the "floodtide." The spirit of God began to speak so emphatically that if we want revival the "leader" is the one who should take the first step. The power of God came on the crowd.

When the invitation was given, the first person to come forward in agony and brokenness was the pastor of that congregation, a deeply spiritual man and highly respected, a spiritual leader, the president of the committee of arrangements, and a man deeply interested in and working for revival. How could such a man stand before a crowd of thousands, including his own congregation, saying, "The fire on my altar is dying out, and I am the hindrance and so I want the Lord to rekindle that fire in my heart."

Temperamentally, he is not a man moved by any wave of emotion, in fact, he speaks against high emotionalism. But he was totally shaken with deep conviction. We praise God for his courage to humble himself. When he knelt at the altar, the whole crowd broke down and began to weep. People who had been fighting against him and trying to get him transferred from there came forward and fell at his feet in brokenness.

What waves of power went through the whole crowd! We felt that the Spirit of God came down in such a mighty way that no one in that great gathering of people could resist Him. One after another people began to stand up and approach the persons whom they had wronged. Some fell on each other's neck and wept. Others fell flat on the ground at the feet of those whom they had wronged.

Certain scenes cannot be described in words. A young man, a teacher in a high school, got up, weeping. He said something like this, "Although I am a Christian, I have hurt my father often and have not respected him as I ought to." He was broken and he crawled with deep conviction to the place where his father was sitting and fell prostrate at his feet and held on to his feet weeping! The father broke down and fell over him. They wept over one another's shoulders and any resentment which was in their hearts flowed out in tears. I could hear the dear man saying to his son, "My son, my son."

A young man came forward and fell at the feet of the pastor. What confession! Another lady came forward and knelt before the pastor in brokenness. She was one of the big opponents of the pastor. But all bitterness was forgotten. The members of the congregation began to be deeply convicted, but the pastor had been broken first. Conviction, confession, and wonderful reconciliation! Not only people in that congregation but people who had come from different places began to stand up confessing their sins, getting reconciled to one another.

When the invitation was given to those who wanted to accept Jesus Christ for the first time, quite a few stood up. Again what joy when we saw sinners come to Christ in repentance. Along with the several who decided for Christ for the first time, all those who already knew Him as their personal Savior were asked to stand up. Almost all the crowd stood up except a few. We began to sing the closing hymn.

Then it happened that a strong young man came running through the crowd to the platform. He wanted to say something. He said something like this. "I am a wicked young man. I have not accepted Christ as my personal Savior, but I cannot resist the Spirit any longer. I accept Him today. I should personally confess to several in this congregation because I have been so wicked, and I have wronged several of you. I want every one of you to forgive me." That was another wave of visitation.

We praise God for this ministry of revival and evangelism that the Lord is graciously helping us to carry on.

Man cannot control the time, the place, or the method God will use in revival. But we are commanded to prepare the way of the Lord (Isa. 40:3–5). God gave a covenant promise to send revival when we fully meet His conditions. "If my people, who are called by my name, will humble themselves and pray and seek my face and turn from their wicked ways, then will I hear from heaven and will forgive their sin and will heal their land" (2 Chron. 7:14).

God has fulfilled this promise thousands of times. He will do so again for you. The more widespread and united the humbling, confession, and prayer—the more widespread the revival God will send. I challenge you to fulfill God's conditions and claim God's promises.

Lord, help me personally to fulfill 2 Chronicles 7:14 today.

Mighty United Intercession

The quickest way to advance the work of God is to advance it on your knees. The deepest foundation that you can lay for revival blessing anywhere is that of prevailing prayer. The mightiest victory that God has ever granted anyone can be yours through prayer. There is no doubt about it—prayer is the key that can unlock any heart, any church, any city, or any nation.

But the prayer that accomplishes such mighty things is not merely a few feeble words uttered occasionally in a half-hearted way after your soul has been blessed by some other Christian's fire. True praying demands more than the occasional hunger of your heart. Prayer must become your constant heart cry. Prayer must become an undying flame on the altar of your soul. It must become the consuming passion of your life. You must saturate your work with intercession.

Mighty personal intercession has closed and opened heaven, according to the prayer of the prophet Elijah. Mighty personal intercession has raised the dead to life at the prayer of the apostle Paul. Mighty personal intercession in the Old Testament times confounded alien armies and routed hostile foes. But the forces of God are engaged today in a spiritual warfare that demands mighty personal intercession plus something more. Nothing less than mighty united intercession will bring to any land or city the needed spiritual awakening. Nothing less will enable the church to complete its unfinished witness to every nation and person. Nothing less will raise up and bring into leadership the mighty prophets needed to shake our land for God. Revival will be born through travail—the travail of the church united in intercession.

Year after year we attend conventions and have our souls rewarmed by the fire of others. Year after year we go empty to special meetings and return filled with new personal blessings. But when will we reach the point where our conventions can help us to reach beyond our personal needs and can launch us into victorious, united intercession for the spiritual needs of our nation and our world? When will we unite on our knees and continue in Holy Spirit intercession until situations have been shaken and changed by divine power (Acts 4:31)?

We all need the supernatural presence of God in all our Christian work. When will we unite in prayer until supernatural power is mightily manifested? If one can chase a thousand but two can put ten thousand to flight (Deut. 32:30), what will be possible when the Christians of our land unite in putting prayer first, unite in days of intercession, and unite in wholesale obedience to the will of God?

What can you do to put prayer first in your work? in your church? What can you do to give prayer its rightful priority in your own life and in the lives of those about you? What step can you take now to lay the foundation for a mighty prayer offensive? We plan for the personnel needed, for adequate literature and programs, and for the financial needs of God's work, but when are we going to begin to plan for the prayer needed? Probably no church or Christian activity is supported by adequate prayer.

Mighty united intercession will not come unless you plan for it. It will not come unless you begin to practice it where you are. Begin with at least one other person. Get a prayer partner. Plan together to put prayer first. Witness to others of the blessings you receive in prayer. Put on the agenda of your next committee meeting the arranging of a plan for a prayer offensive in your ministry or church. Is anything more important?

Do you want to see a new day dawn in your city? Are you willing to put prayer first in your personal life and in your plans for your outreach? Revival can come to your church or city this year if you meet God's conditions.

Lord, unite us Christians in prayer for revival.

Over Which Cities Do You Weep?

As Jesus neared Jerusalem at the beginning of His triumphal entry, He was coming from Bethany. He rounded the corner of Olivet and as the path descended toward the city, He saw the full panorama of Jerusalem. A great company of disciples and Galileans were with Him. The disciples and the crowd had been shouting enthusiastically and joyfully, "Blessed is the king who comes in the name of the Lord! Peace in heaven and glory in the highest!" (Luke 19:37–38).

To the amazement of all, Jesus burst into loud weeping as the tears coursed down His cheeks. Luke does not use the ordinary word for weeping but the strongest available Greek word, which expresses the loud cry of a soul in agony. This was the city Jesus loved so well, for which He was gladly willing to die. His very soul burst out in an agony of tears and heart cries. He loved Jerusalem so much, but Jerusalem would not accept His love.

The tears of Jesus are the tears of God the Father and God the Holy Spirit. The loud, agonizing cry of Jesus shows the agony of the Triune God. This is not the only time Jesus wept in agony. Hear the words of Luke 13:34, "O Jerusalem, Jerusalem . . . how often I have longed to gather your children together, as a hen gathers her chicks under her wings, but you were not willing!"

Earlier, when He went through the towns and villages of Galilee teaching, preaching, and healing, we read that when He saw the crowds He was moved with compassion for them because they were like sheep without a shepherd (Matt. 9:35–36). This is the same compassion that caused God to be concerned and to love the great city of Nineveh even though it was the enemy of His people (Jonah 4:11). God loves the people of each city, whether it be His chosen city of Jerusalem or the great enemy city of Nineveh. God's heart has the same love for all.

The Jesus who wept over Jerusalem weeps over our cities today. Do you? Jesus weeps over the cities because so many people live there, so many whom He loves with infinite yet personal love. He longs to save them. He died for them. Yet they go on in their sin. God hates sin, but He loves the sinner. God is angry with Satan as he deceives and destroys people through sin. But God's heart cries out in love and mercy to each sinner. He does not want anyone to perish but desires that everyone come to repentance (2 Peter 3:9).

Do you remember the deeply moving picture of God's loving, seeking, longing heart in Isaiah 65:1–2? It should be ever in your memory. "To a nation that did not call on my name, I said, 'Here am I, here am I.' All day long I have held out my hands to an obstinate people." Do you see Him? Can you see Him? Jesus stands looking down on our cities, on our crowded streets, on the multitude of our homes. He sees people so full of need, yet turning everywhere else for help except to Him. In loving longing, with arms outstretched, He cries out to them, "Here I am, here I am."

The true picture of our God is of one who stands in our cities with His arms outstretched hour after hour, day after day. He wants to welcome us. He wants to receive us. All day long He reaches out to us. All day long He calls, "Here I am! Here I am!" But people go on heedlessly in their own ways. They do not see Him. They do not hear His voice. They are not calling on His name, but He is calling to them. People are seeking fun, pleasure, money, possessions, position, and power. But when they find any or all of these, their hearts are still empty. How often Jesus weeps as we forget Him, disregard Him, and grieve Him.

Do you love people enough to weep over them? You may not have an actual tear in your eye, though I hope you do. But at least your heart can weep for the unsaved and the spiritually lost. We used to sing the gospel hymn by Thomas Shepherd that begins with this stanza:

> *Must Jesus bear the cross alone*
> *And all the world go free?*
> *No; there's a cross for everyone,*
> *And there's a cross for me!*

Jesus is waiting for your heart to weep. Which cities are you willing to take on your heart until you feel the tears of the heart of God? Do you weep over your own city? over New York? Tokyo? Moscow? Mexico City? Blessed are those who carry a prayer burden for several of earth's cities with their teeming masses of needy, hurting, and lost people. Blessed are you if you cry out to God each day with a hungry heart for God's saving work in at least one or two cities.

I well remember sixty years ago when I went to Bible college and heard the young man across the hall in my dormitory weep evening after evening as he prayed. He would look out of his window over our city. Again and again I could hear him sobbing and weeping in his room for the sinful people living in the streets and homes of that city. He prayed for them and loved them and longed for their salvation.

Do you know what it is to carry a prayer burden for others? Do you know what it is to weep in loving longing for the salvation of loved ones and friends? I plead with you, take some city to your heart. Begin to pray and weep with longing over one or more of the great cities on the mission fields. You will thrill the heart of God if you do. He wants to love the cities and their people through your heart and your prayers.

∞

Lord, place a prayer burden on my heart for the city of

_____.

Where Are Your Tears?

There are tears in the sinner's eyes.
Habits of sin binding heart, hand, and feet;
Broken with shame at his sin and defeat,
Hot burning tears coursing down his hot cheek—
There are tears in the sinner's eyes.

There are tears in the suff'rer's eyes.
Long weary hours of disease, weakness, pain,
Praying that health be restored once again,
Waiting for healing, but waiting in vain—
There are tears in the suff'rer's eyes.

There are tears in discouraged eyes.
Misunderstood by the ones who should know;
No one to love, to compassion bestow,
Fainting, discouraged, with hope burning low—
There are tears in discouraged eyes.

There are tears in non-Christian eyes.
Calling to idols of wood and of stone,
Calling in vain, Christ the Savior unknown,
Comfortless, helpless, without God, alone—
There are tears in non-Christian eyes.

There are tears in the Savior's eyes.
Tears for those sinning, discouraged, and ill,
Tears for the straying ones, out of His will,
Tears for the millions unreached by us still—
There are tears in the Savior's eyes.

But where are the tears in your eyes?
Can you not weep with the millions who weep?
Have you no tears for the other lost sheep?
Jesus is weeping! Are you still asleep?
OH! WHERE ARE THE TEARS IN YOUR EYES?

                                        Wesley L. Duewel

The Holy Spirit and Teams

The Holy Spirit-given pattern for Christian work in this dispensation is not that of one-man authoritarian leadership or benevolent spiritual dictatorship. His inspired pattern is that of group leadership—that is, committee leadership with fellowship in responsibility and guidance. The Lord did not entrust the early church entirely to Peter or John; He saw to it that there were twelve apostles. And the early apostolic chairman surprisingly was James. The apostles seemed to make it a point to set apart or ordain plural leadership in the individual churches they formed.

God still raises up a minimum number of spiritual giants with specialized ministries. These always function better as leaders of a closely knit group. A Paul or a Billy Graham needs a team. Paul received a vision in the night, but his team was able to refer to the guidance he received in this way: "We got ready at once . . . concluding that God had called us" (Acts 16:10).

A leader who dominates a committee that always says yes to his ideas proves that both he and they have substituted man's leadership for the leadership of the Holy Spirit.

From the earliest days to the present, whenever God has worked in mighty revival power, He has repeatedly given guidance and assigned steps of obedience to unexpected members of groups. Thus no person can glory in His presence. Too often, groups that make remarkable claims of spirituality have been marked by dictatorial tendencies and authoritarian ways.

The Holy Spirit-given pattern for Christian work is seldom individualistic. The Christian "freelance" worker is usually a maladjusted person who has previously been a problem to fellow workers. He may have a great devotion to Christ in his own way, but he usually has God's second best for his life. God in His graciousness will continue to make him a blessing in many ways—but the more God is able to use him, in spite of his angularity, the more this is proof of how greatly God could use him if he were spiritually pliable and mature.

Such individualists are always problems to God and man. They usually have difficulty in one or more of the following ways: in getting the guidance of the Spirit; in holding steady in unspectacular and essential, though apparently fruitless places; and in adjusting to their fellow Christian workers.

They often have a record of being in and out of more than one organization. They do not trust the Holy Spirit to guide others. They may think God has "thrust" them out; actually they have shut themselves out. Spirituality is not synonymous with pliability and adjustability, but there is a very close relation between them, according to 1 Corinthians 13.

God asks that normally His pastors be family men with a well-adjusted family life. Christ sent His young disciples out by twos. The Holy Spirit asked the church to set apart Paul and Barnabas as a team, knowing that both needed for a time the discipline of close fellowship with someone of a strikingly different personality.

The individual on his own gets too accustomed to having his own way, to feeling that the Lord guides the church through him rather than through others. Becoming set in his own ways, he becomes less sensitive to the manifoldness of the ways in which the Spirit operates. He becomes intolerant of others' ways and opinions. He shows great piety as long as he is in the position of leadership, but he is extremely restless, if not carnal, if he has to follow the leadership of others.

Spirituality shows best in group situations. Patience, humility, forbearance, and love shine brightest in the give-and-take of close-working groups. Christlikeness is not best measured in the pulpit, but in the home, in committees, and in the pressures of group and institutional life. You are not spiritually mature and ready for heaven's fellowship until you can delight to say "not I but Christ" in all types of group associations and pressures.

Lord, help me always to work well with others.

Put Praise First

God wants you to put praise first. Nothing is more blessed, nothing is more neglected, nothing is more urgent. Christian life can be transformed when praise is put first. Christian service can be endued with new power when praise fills the heart. Christian warfare can be turned into triumphant conquest when praise leads the way. We need to do something about putting praise first.

We must never separate prayer and praise. Prayer and praise are the two wings by which our souls mount into heaven. If either one is neglected, we fail to soar on wings like eagles (Isa. 40:31). Prayer and praise are the two steps by which the army of the Lord marches forward. As surely as soldiers march always "left, right, left, right," so we must keep our praising as up-to-date as our praying if we want to advance for God. We are all in danger of neglecting prayer, and perhaps we are all in even greater danger of neglecting praise. Many a prayer meeting would come to new life and power if people began to praise the Lord.

If there is anything that is a better measure of the spiritual life than the prayer life, it is the praise life. Satan fears prayer, but if there is anything Satan fears more than prayer, it is praise. God waits to hear the voices of His children. It is the sweetest of music to His ear. If there is anything He delights to hear more than the voice of prayer and intercession, it is the voice of praise and adoration.

Prayer adds its sweet perfume to the Christian's life, but if there is anything that makes the Christian's life even more fragrant, it is praise. It is not a question of prayer or praise—we must keep the two together. If we are to pray without ceasing, much of the time should be given to praise.

Praise makes the soul beautiful. It is perhaps the most heavenly activity in which the soul can engage. A life filled with praise becomes almost angelic. Praise, thanksgiving, love, and adoration—these make the life radiant. The Holy Spirit shines through the Christian's life that is saturated with praise. The Shekinah glory of God marks the life that rejoices evermore, gives thanks in everything, and radiates pure love for God and others. Praise adds sweetness to the voice and loveliness to the soul. Praise fills the life with song, the heart with joy, and adds a graciousness to all of life. Praise clothes a life with heaven's beauty.

Praise opens the gates to blessing. Praise needs literally to be put first in prayer. It is significant that in the future glory, when our walls are "Salvation," our gates will be "Praise" (Isa. 60:18). "Enter his gates with thanksgiving and his courts with praise" (Ps. 100:4). There is no more worthy entrance into the presence of God than the entrance of praise. Praise opens the gates to blessing. Praise opens the way to answered prayer. Praise opens the way to the very heart of God.

Praise increases the presence and power of the Lord. It is a fact of the blessed life that praise not merely adds blessing but also increases every blessing of God. Praise fills the life with the atmosphere of heaven. There are times when it is not easy to praise. There are times when it is easier to pray than to praise. But "through Jesus . . . let us continually offer to God a sacrifice of praise" (Heb. 13:15).

When you begin to praise, the disquiet of your heart and your restlessness and fear begin to disappear like fog before sunshine. When you begin to praise, peace is blessedly multiplied and sorrow is turned to joy. When you begin to praise, grumbling and criticism wither at the roots, the breath of heaven blows the cloud away, and you feel clean and new again. When you begin to praise, Satan turns in terror and soon flees.

Praising God opens your heart to God and to all His sweet heavenly influences. It gives the Holy Spirit a welcome and access to your life and lifts you above the trivial accusations of Satan. Praising God reduces your problem mountains into hills of blessing. Praising God gives you the eagle's vision and by the eye of faith you see the victory ahead.

Praising God multiplies your faith and fills you "with all joy and peace as you trust in him, so that you may overflow with hope by the power of the Holy Spirit" (Rom. 15:13). Praising God seems to fill you with the very faith of God and to strengthen you with the power of the Holy Spirit. Praising God changes you and changes the situation before you; it opens the way to miracle.

Praising God makes you triumphant in the battle, bringing to your aid all the resources of heaven. The angels of God recognize the sound of praise and rush to your side to win the victory for God. Praising God brings the shout of victory in the midst of the battle and turns the battle into a rout of the enemy.

In a battle in the time of Jehoshaphat when the king and people humbled themselves and sought God's face, He put His Spirit on an unknown Levite, and through him God gave them a message of hope. They believed the promise of God and marched into battle with singers praising God in front of the battle troops. "As they began to sing and praise, the Lord set ambushes" (2 Chron. 20:22).

Praise sets an ambush for the Devil; no wonder he flees at the sound of praise! When Israel praised God, the walls of Jericho fell down. When Paul and Silas praised and sang, the Lord shook open the gates of the jail at Philippi. And when you begin to praise the Lord, new victories will dawn for you.

This was the secret that David learned, and we all need to learn it over and over. Listen to him testify, "I will extol the Lord at all times; his praise will always be on my lips" (Ps. 34:1). "My tongue will speak of . . . your praises all day long" (35:28). "My mouth is filled with your praise . . . all day" (71:8). "Who can . . . fully declare his praise?" (106:2). "As for me, I will always have hope; I will praise you more and more" (71:14). Can you not see why David was a man after God's own heart?

Let us make our life a life of praise. Begin by making this day a day of praise. Begin by filling your heart with God's praises wherever you go. Begin by praising the Lord the first thing each morning. Begin by praising God every time you feel tempted to doubt, to fear, to worry, to criticize, or to yield to any kind of temptation. Praise fills you with faith and power. Praise clothes you with heaven's beauty. Praise opens the gates to blessing. Praise wins the battle for God. "Praise the Lord, O my soul. I will praise the Lord all my life; I will sing praise to my God as long as I live" (Ps. 146:1–2).

Lord, may my praise give You daily joy.

Lessons from the Graham Crusades

For almost fifty years God has been using Dr. Billy Graham and his team to call people, cities, and even nations back to God. Nearly fifty years ago, in the early days of the team, I wrote observations that have been validated repeatedly over the years since then. May God use these pointers to guide us as we seek revival and harvest today.

In 1955, during the all-Scotland crusade, many observed that never had Scotland been so saturated with prayer. They knew of twenty thousand prayer partners around the world who were praying daily for the crusade. In many countries, on ships at sea, in homes and gospel halls, in church buildings people were gathering together to pray. Hundreds of letters, telegrams, and cables arrived daily from distant places assuring the team of prayer. For example, every morning four hundred leprosy patients in Africa met to pray. Night after night hundreds of prayer groups around the world sought God's blessing for Scotland. Indeed, there were many all-night prayer meetings.

Why should we be surprised when God answers prayer and fulfills His promises? The potential blessing that can be poured out when thousands of God's people unite in prayer is almost unbelievable. We do not earn God's blessing by prayer, but we drive back the powers of darkness, and we prepare the way of the Lord. God has covenanted to work and answer prayer when His people unitedly seek His face.

The many thousands of recorded decisions over nearly fifty years of Graham crusades are God's evidence that He answers prayer. Not everyone who made a commitment in a crusade has maintained that commitment to Christ, but, thank God, thousands have. You can meet them in thousands of churches. Hundreds and hundreds of ministers and missionaries who are in God's work today testify that God moved them during a Billy Graham crusade.

Often in halls in distant cities, where the crusade services were carried by phone lines, the results were even greater than they were in the great auditoriums where Billy Graham himself was present and speaking. The glory does not go to the evangelist, to his team, or to the wonderfully organized cooperation of many people and churches, but to the God who answers prayer.

When will we learn this lesson: If God's people will truly unite in prevailing prayer, nothing is too difficult for God. When the church travails in prayer, God answers. When sufficient prayer is concentrated on any work, on your work, God will do the miracle. Often your most important task is to enlist adequate prayer and to pray faithfully yourself.

God gives grace to the humble. Perhaps a second outstanding lesson of the crusades is that there is no limit to what God will do for those who are humble. Humility would seem to be most difficult in such widely advertised mass campaigns. But the campaigns have shown us that God can bless the widely advertised efforts. God does not despise the use of modern equipment and techniques, provided there is adequate prayer and humility. God does not cease to work just because His instrument becomes widely known and much loved, provided that person remains absolutely hidden behind the Cross. By their true humility all the Billy Graham crusade teams have repeatedly impressed those who work with them. The most bitter opponents have been won to friendship and to Christ by the evident sincerity and humility that they observed. Newspaper reporters have come to respect the team and many have experienced new birth in Christ. In Scotland, a Christian newsman's fellowship was organized as a result of the crusade. Yes, the widest publicity is compatible with the deepest humility.

Billy Graham repeatedly urged, "Forget me; if you get your eyes on me, this crusade will fail." He has pleaded for prayer lest God remove His hand from his life and cease to use him. He repeatedly said that any one of five hundred preachers in Scotland could preach better than he. He said on one occasion that he would be nothing but a dead stick of wood if God removed His hand from him.

His team members are normal human beings, but they love the Lord. For all these years God has helped them to remain bound together with cords of love, mutual respect, and humility. A close friend of mine, who traveled with the team for one month across India, saw them intimately in their casual moments as well as on the platform before thousands of people. His report was that it was beautiful to see the unity, the humility, and the prayerfulness of the team.

How much do we as gospel workers know of real humility? How much do we know of becoming absolutely nothing that Christ may be all? Perhaps the biggest hindrance to God's work and to God's using us mightily is our pride—pride about our institutions, our churches, our schools, our hard work, even our beliefs and professed spirituality. God help us to learn the full meaning of giving Him all the glory.

The lesson of the crusades over the years has been that there is no limit to what God will do for you if you pray enough and if you are small enough and humble enough for Him to use.

Lord, teach us that there is no substitute for prayer and humility.

Will You Pay the Cost?

What price are you willing to pay? Nothing we can ever do can earn God's blessing—every work of God and every good gift is by His infinite grace (James 1:17). Nevertheless every movement of God in which we are called to have a part involves a cost. God has chosen it to be so. It is of God's grace that He has called us to be His co-workers. It is His grace that honors us with a share in paying the cost of the salvation of people and the advance of His kingdom. What cost are you willing to pay?

Blessing is costly. Only God could pay the infinite price that made our salvation possible. There was an infinite cost to God the Father. Was it a trivial matter for God the Father to see God the Son depart from heaven on His redemptive mission to earth? Was it trivial for God the Father to turn His back on His Son and to let His Son feel the fullness of divine wrath for sin as He bore the sins of the world? He who thinks this has never understood the heart of a father, nor the heart of God. The whole Trinity paid an infinite cost in redemption at the Cross. God's price is paid. It is finished.

Today there is a cost for you and me to pay. There was a price to pay in Paul's day, and he gladly paid it (Col. 1:24; see also 2 Cor. 11:23–28). There is a price to be paid today. Every age demands new sacrifice. Every day sees a new cost being paid. The victories of God and His kingdom do not come cheaply at any time.

No generation is ever moved for God without great cost being paid. No great revival is obtained at a bargain sale. No mighty awakening is born without hidden travail. There are no shortcuts to miracle. There is no Pentecost without a Calvary.

God's work is hindered today by the shortage of God's children willing to pay a high price. It was true in Isaiah's day. The Triune God was waiting for someone to do and go (Isa. 6:8). It was true in Ezekiel's day. God was searching for someone to stand in the gap and hold back the sins that were destroying the land and calling for God's judgment (Ezek. 22:30). It was true in Paul's day. The apostle often seemed to be alone in the battle for souls; most others seemed to be seeking their own interests, their own advantage, their own comfort (Phil. 2:20–21; 2 Tim. 4:9–11). It is true today. The majority of Christians are nominal; they do not know there is a price to pay. The majority of spiritual Christians are sleeping; they are unaware of the cost they could and should be paying.

We are faced today with spiritual shortages. There is a reason that in spite of many encouragements the mighty revival movement of God for which we long is not yet here. There is no shortage with God. God's resurrection power is still mightily at work in wonderful ways. There is no dispensational problem. This is still the day of grace, the dispensation of the Spirit. He is here in all His miracle working, in conviction, conversion, sanctification, and revival. This is the dispensation of "times of refreshing," of outpourings of the Holy Spirit (Acts 3:19).

Nevertheless, great spiritual need exists. Gracious blessings are many, but the mightier movements of God are few. The hymn goes "Mercy-drops 'round us are falling, but for the showers we plead." Good Christians are perhaps more numerous than ever before, but giants of God are few. Wistful well-wishers of revival are numerous among spiritual people, but great price-payers are few.

Spiritual shortages are great. There is a shortage of prolonged praying. There is a shortage of fasting. Much seed is sown, but little is sown with tears, and hence there is comparatively little reaping (Ps. 126:5). There is a lot of talk about "accepting Jesus" but little about taking up one's cross. There is a shortage of mountain-moving faith. There is a shortage of men and women who know how to wrestle in prayer (Col. 4:12). Prayer is for most people a casual social conversation with Jesus, not a Gethsemane-shared intercession.

Your part has probably been good—good, but ordinary. You have probably not crucified Christ afresh by blatant, overt sins, but has Christ often had to say to you, "Are you still sleeping and resting? Look, the hour is near" (Matt. 26:45)? In all probability your tomorrow will be much like your past. It is all too easy to make excuses.

There are too many reasons why you may continue much the same as you have been living! You are too busy to pay a great price! You can't afford it! Prices are high! It would cost part of the time you want to visit with friends. It would cost part of the time you spend reading the newspaper or watching TV. It might cost some of your mealtimes to fast and pray. It could cost some of your habits, your hobbies, and part of your work that till now you have thought no one else could do.

The cost is very great! But I challenge you to pay the price regardless of the cost. I challenge you to really make some radical changes in your life in order to put prayer and Christ's kingdom first. I challenge you to choose Gethsemane. I challenge you to put your prayer closet before yourself, your appearance, your friends, your work. I challenge you to do something drastic and definite. Will you pay the price now? or never?

Lord, in mercy wake me up. Don't let me fail You.

Your Biography in Heaven 52

Your life is being recorded day by day in heaven. In heaven's library, there is a book being written that has your name on the cover. God has planned that the records of all of our lives be preserved. Angels gather and record all the facts of your thought life—your ambitions, your hopes, your prayers, your intentions, your motives, your efforts, your carefulness or your carelessness. All your words, all your deeds, all your prayers, all your love or the opposite—all have been recorded.

Your record in heaven is already quite extensive. Your life is recorded from earth's details but from heaven's perspective. The record of each day is complete.

You may think that little happened in your life today, but you are spending a full twenty-four hours. Most of it may have been comparatively trivial. If so, that is what heaven's record will record. Was most of today wasted or invested?

Today's account of your life will be recorded as time invested or lost, opportunities seized and added to your investment, or opportunities lost with resulting eternal loss to you (1 Cor. 3:14–15). My book *Measure Your Life* emphasizes the importance of evaluating your life from God's—that is, eternity's—perspective.

Your minutes and hours, whether at work, at home, at school, or at church; whether for yourself, for your family, or for others; whether for your nation, for the kingdom of God, or for Jesus' sake—all are either investments that will be rewarded or a loss forever. Many of the events of your life you have already forgotten, but all the events have been faithfully recorded by the angels. Times when you heard of another Christian in need and your heart immediately reached out to that person in Christian love and you prayed specially for him or her are all recorded. The times when you prayed for the unsaved people in your community, for God to restrain crime or to help guilty criminals to be found and arrested, times when you prayed for justice to be done in the courts—all are recorded. The time you spent praying for the schools of your community and the churches of your community are all recorded—unless you failed to pray.

Your record includes your faithfulness in praying for the salvation of your president and his family; for God's guidance in his speeches, decisions, and actions; for God to restrain him from making wrong decisions and taking wrong positions on crucial issues. Since the Bible commands you to thank God and pray for every person, especially those in authority over you (1 Tim. 2:1–3), your faithfulness in praying for your mayor, governor, senators, congressmen, Supreme Court justices, and others in responsible positions is an important part of your life's history. If you have not prayed for these leaders, your lack of praying is recorded as a blank and a loss.

Your prayer investment in evangelistic campaigns in your city or church and in the radio and TV ministry of the people God is using have been recorded. Your heart cries for people hurt in accidents, for people bereaved by tragedy, for peace among the warring groups in other nations have been recorded—if you prayed about them. If you didn't pray, the lack speaks eloquently of the lack in your spiritual life or of your disregard for your spiritual opportunities.

Your biography is important to God because He is planning wonderful rewards for you throughout eternity. These rewards will be in strict accord with the record of your life. How much did you long for God to bless others? How much did you pray for many aspects of Christ's kingdom? How many names did you include in your prayer list because you were seeking to please Him and to help others? God's rewards will be complete and in perfect accord with your record.

No human biography is ever complete because no biographer ever knows all of a person's thoughts, motives, hopes, and desires except as they can be informed from what is seen or heard. But heaven's records will be complete. They will include all your actions, words, thoughts, hopes and desires, plans, prayers, fears, memories, understandings, misunderstandings, joys, and sorrows. Only an infinite God can be the final judge of anyone's life on earth because only He can take into consideration all these many, many aspects that are important to the evaluation of your life. Only He can understand, remember, and integrate it all in rendering His decision about your rewards.

Will your record have only one use—at the Judgment Day? Of course not. Most probably, in eternity you will want to look back and refresh your memory repeatedly of many events that you have long forgotten. No doubt you will want to know who blessed you, who prayed for you, who strengthened you by their prayers. You will want to thank many people for blessings that you received through their love and prayer, though you had never realized it before.

You will be able to research things for which you always wanted answers—why some answers to prayer were delayed, why some prayers were denied. You will be amazed to see how merciful God was not to answer some of your prayers and how much wiser God's way was compared to your short-sighted desire.

You will be amazed at the perfect detail in which all your loving thoughts of others, all your holy desires for others, all your thankful appreciation of others is recorded. I hope your prayer records are so extensive and so detailed that you will be amazed at how your prayers brought blessings, encouragement, and help to many, many people. How gloriously God will reward you! With what thankfulness, love, and honor those for whom you prayed will greet you!

But oh! how many Christians will have short records of their prayer lives! Then they will be aware of how often they merely enjoyed life for themselves, how little they cared about, thought of, and prayed for others.

Paul described how Epaphras, pastor at the church at Colosse, labored in prayer. When he stayed with Paul for some months to help and encourage him, Paul reported that he had an extensive prayer life for the Christians at Colosse, Laodicea, and Hierapolis (Col. 4:12–13). Paul describes it thus: "He is always wrestling in prayer for you, that you may stand firm in all the will of God, mature and fully assured. I vouch for him that he is working hard for you and for those at Laodicea and Hierapolis."

I wonder how embarrassed some pastors will be when their congregations discover how little their pastors actually prayed for them. Did they really, in the words of Paul, labor and work hard in their prayers? I fear many will not be among the prayer heroes of eternity.

Will there be something similar to but much, much superior to computers in eternity? I think there may well be. Undoubtedly God has a wonderful way to keep the millions of complete records of the lives of His children, and I believe we will have access to many of these wonderful, inspiring, and God-glorifying biographies, histories, and records.

Does God have video-type records of your life? I don't doubt it in the least. However, these records will be far superior to anything we have seen on earth. From time to time someone who was drowning or was in a terrifying accident has described how in almost a moment of time much of his life passed before him in his mind's eye. Were all those vivid memories stored in his own brain? Perhaps. What an amazing mind we have! Or did God cause some kind of a momentary replay of the records He has? Who knows?

No doubt there will be all kinds of concerts and musical presentations in heaven. Surely we shall have great thrilling congregational singing. Will some of your favorite hymns be translated into the language of heaven and sung there?

Think of the dramatic presentations of the life stories of both famous and hidden saints, evangelists of the cross, missionaries, prophets, and apostles! Think of the "This is Your Life" type of presentation for Joseph, David, Hezekiah, the apostles John and Paul, Luther, John Wesley, and you! These presentations may possibly close with a question-and-answer period. Then you will get some of your questions answered that you have long wished you could ask these saints.

Will angels want to present your life story, part of it or all of it? Your biography in heaven will furnish lots of material. Think! The record of your prayer life this week too will be part of your record there, for you are furnishing materials each day for your heavenly records. You cannot change one thing that has already been recorded. Sins forgiven will be erased from God's record, but there will still be a record of every day of your life.

Today you have the opportunity to decide what will be the record for the rest of your life, for what your prayer life will be tomorrow. Today you are privileged to invest your love and your time in a thousand ways for eternity. Will you change? Will you open your life to God anew and truly begin to invest for eternity? The decision is in your hand.

Lord, "teach us to number our days aright, that we may gain a heart of wisdom" (Ps. 90:12).

Index of Themes

If God has made this book a blessing to you and you wish to share a testimony, or if you wish the author to remember you in a moment of prayer, feel free to write:

Dr. Wesley L. Duewel
P.O. Box A
Greenwood, IN 46142-6599